A SEPARATE CINEMA

A SEPARATE CINEMA

FIFTY YEARS OF BLACK-CAST POSTERS

JOHN KISCH AND EDWARD MAPP

PREFACE BY SPIKE LEE

INTRODUCTION BY DONALD BOGLE

THE NOONDAY PRESS

FARRAR, STRAUS AND GIROUX

NEW YORK

Copyright © 1992 by John Kisch and Edward Mapp
Introduction copyright © 1992 by Donald Bogle
Preface copyright © 1992 by Spike Lee
All rights reserved
Designed by Debbie Glasserman
Separations by Hongkong Scanner Craft Corporation
Printed and bound at Arcata Graphics, Kingsport, TN
First edition, 1992

Library of Congress Cataloging-in-Publication Data
Kisch, John.
A separate cinema: fifty years of black-cast posters / John Kisch
and Edward Mapp; preface by Spike Lee; introduction by Donald Bogle.
p.   cm.
Includes index.
1. Film posters, American.   2. Afro-Americans in motion pictures.
3. Motion pictures—United States—History.   I. Mapp, Edward.
II. Title.
PN1995.9.P5K57   1992   791.43′028′089960773—dc20   92-15037   CIP

Excerpts from *Amateur Night at the Apollo* by Ralph Cooper. Copyright © 1991 by Ralph Cooper Literary, Inc. Reprinted by permission of HarperCollins Publishers Inc.

Excerpt from *Lena* by Lena Horne and Richard Schickel, copyright © 1965 by Lena Horne and Richard Schickel, reprinted by permission of Doubleday, a division of Bantam Doubleday Dell Publishing Group, Inc.

Excerpts from "The Shadow and the Act" in *Shadow and Act* by Ralph Ellison, copyright © 1972 by Ralph Ellison, reprinted by permission of Random House, Inc.

Josephine BAKER

PRINSESSE TAM·TAM
DEN SORTE REVYDRONNING I EN NY STRAALENDE FILM
MED **ALBERT PREJEAN**
ISCENESAT AF: EDMOND GREVILLE   MUSIK: JACQUES DALLIN

3 BERØMTE PARISISKE JAZZORKESTRE SPILLER I DENNE STORFILM

CONTENTS

CONTENTS

This book is right on time, coinciding with the new Black Wave in Cinema. I've been looking for this book, waiting for this book a long, long time. Even before I wanted to be a filmmaker, when I was a mere youth, I collected stuff. First, it was comic books, baseball cards; then I moved on to collecting autographs. You see, I've always been a collector. Once I began to make films, I started to amass film memorabilia—in particular, black films. So you can understand my delight in this fine-looking, fully researched, and also fun book. Let's all nod in appreciation to Donald Bogle for his essay, for putting everything in historical perspective. Mr. Bogle continues to be our most noted black-cinema historian. And let me thank John Kisch and Edward Mapp. It's about time we as a people started to document our past, our history.

In closing, I'm happy to say I own copies of several of the one-sheet posters seen in this book. There are a lot more that I want to get. Our cinematic history must be preserved.

—Spike Lee
Brooklyn, New York

"Things ain't what they used to be."

Duke and Mercer Ellington

In Oscar Micheaux's *Underworld*, Bee Freeman plays Dinah. She's a headstrong, feisty, sexy, and resolutely independent woman who is accustomed to calling the shots and, if necessary, to putting men in their place. She struts, strolls, connives, commands, and causes havoc for her naïve good-boy lover, Paul, who does not seem to understand that with Dinah, he's way out of his league. Dinah gets the poor guy framed for murder. Some might see her as a woman scorned, others simply as the classic screen bitch. Regardless, by the climax of *Underworld*, Dinah suffers a fate frequently reserved for independent ambitious screen heroines of the past. A speeding train collides with the car she is driving, and thus poor Dinah dies a wicked death—in punishment, of course, for her *wicked* aggressiveness.

Underworld is a mangled film. Technically choppy and disjointed, its plot seems to roam all over the place. But like its spirited heroine, the film grasps our attention. It's a race movie, one of several hundred black-cast motion pictures made especially for African-American audiences and independently produced outside the Hollywood system. As such, it is but one episode in the long, sometimes contradictory and complex, and far too often overlooked history of blacks in American movies during the first half of the century.

Contrary to what many today may believe, black images and performers in the movies are nothing new; they have been an integral part of American cinema almost from its beginnings. In some respects, early black movie history falls into two distinct categories, with two vastly different perspectives and identities.

On one side are the race movies, which flourished from the teens into the late 1940s. Here, away from the big Hollywood studios and working on tight, limited budgets, independent filmmakers—some black, others white—sought to provide mass entertainment for a black audience by creating stories with distinct cultural references, signs, and signposts; by dramatizing worlds in which African-American heroes and heroines were depicted as vital, ambitious, assertive protagonists.

On the other side of this early history are the images and performers that reached audiences by way of Hollywood. Here, in technically polished and well-crafted products, individual African-American actors and actresses found themselves saddled with stereotyped roles. Yet surprisingly enough, many managed to flip the stereotyped images inside out and to come up with highly idiosyncratic and fascinating work that can still excite audiences.

THE EARLY YEARS

No doubt the most disturbing African-American images are the early ones. In short films created by whites in an evolving film industry during the dawning years of the century, all audiences could expect to see of black America was a steady lineup of stereotypes. In such early movie shorts as *Wooing and Wedding of a Coon* (1905), *The Dancing Nig* (1907), *For Massa's Sake* (1911), and the Rastus series (*How Rastus Got His Turkey*, *Rastus' Riotous Ride*, and *How Rastus Got His Chicken*, c. 1910–11), a troupe of crude, insulting, racist images stumbled across the screen: dimwitted, comic, contorted coons; loyal, submissive, doltish toms; bossy and overbearing or joyous and cheery mammies. Worse, often enough, the black roles were mostly played by whites in blackface, making the characters all the more grotesque and alien.

Of course, American movies did not create these stereotypes; such images had been around since the white minstrel shows of the nineteenth century. Indeed, for white America, they represented an accepted way of looking at African-Americans. The stereotypes eased white tensions

Tin Ghost *(1926)*

about black America and put to rest any concern about social/ racial inequities and injustices; at the same time, the images served to justify notions of white superiority and power. Once these already popular stereotypes were put on film, however, they reached a far broader audience with a far greater social/ political impact.

During this early period, no images of blacks in film proved more shocking than those in D. W. Griffith's now legendary, racist masterpiece, *The Birth of a Nation* (1915). In this drama, which focuses on the Old South, the Civil War, and the Reconstruction Era, Griffith depicted his black characters as either gentle, loyal servants or fiery renegades, lusting for power and, worse still, the flesh of white women. In one memorable sequence, a renegade black pursues a fragile young white woman. Terrified, but refusing to submit to him, and determined to keep her honor, she runs to a cliff and throws herself off.

Perhaps no other film in movie history has ever quite as powerfully articulated a particular white American nightmare:

fear of black male sexuality and aggression. And perhaps no other film has ever so shockingly sought to dramatize a restoration of order to a world in which one race has forgotten its place: *The Birth of a Nation* climaxes with a group of stalwart upright white males wearing sheets and hoods. It becomes an unabashed tribute to the Klan.

Nonetheless, dazzled by Griffith's technical innovations, his powerful use of this new medium, and his race theme, white audiences flocked to see *The Birth of a Nation*. It was an unqualified hit, one of the most successful motion pictures in history. Among those praising the film was President Woodrow Wilson. With the release of *The Birth of a Nation*, Ralph Ellison wrote in his essay "The Shadow and the Act," "the propagation of subhuman images of Negroes became financially and dramatically profitable. The Negro as scapegoat could be sold as entertainment, could even be exported. If the film became the main manipulator of the American dream, for Negroes that dream contained a strong dose of such stuff as nightmares are made of."

African-American leaders were outraged. The NAACP launched a formal protest against the film in an effort to have it banned and boycotted. But something else also happened. By 1912, an African-American by the name of William Foster had already started making his own short black comedies in Chicago. Now, in part fired up by a drive to counteract the racism of *The Birth of a Nation*, there appeared the first group of independent African-American filmmakers, who, realizing the power of this new medium, sought to make their own motion pictures. They scrambled for money (from the black bourgeoisie or white backers) and quickly formed production companies.

INDEPENDENT FEVER: EARLY RACE CINEMA

Among the early independents were Emmett J. Scott, who gathered funds to launch an ill-fated production, *The Birth of a Race* (ca. 1918); the brothers Noble and George Johnson, who formed the Lincoln Motion Picture Company to produce such films as *The Realization of a Negro's Ambition* (1916) and *Trooper of Troop K* (1916); and director Oscar Micheaux, who, in 1918, directed his first film, *The Homesteader*. Initially, all these early figures hoped to make movies of racial uplift and inspiration, tributes to black endurance and ambition. They remain important mainly because they proved that African-American cinema could exist.

Soon other film companies (Reol Productions, the Unique Film Company, the Norman Film Manufacturing Company, the Frederick Douglass Film Company), some black-owned, others white-controlled, shot up in places as diverse as Jacksonville, Florida, St. Louis, Philadelphia, Chicago, and New York, sometimes using the abandoned studios of mainstream film companies that had fled to California. They turned out black-cast race movies, which were shown at big-city ghetto movie houses in the North, at segregated theaters in the South, and, on occasion, at black churches, schools, and social gatherings. By some estimates, before this movement of independents ended, approximately 150 such companies had come into existence. Of these, about a third were black.

The race movies varied in style, technique, and subject matter. Sometimes plodding, sometimes didactic, sometimes deliriously disjointed, often the race films were, quite frankly, terrible.

Others offered rousing, optimistic visions of black derring-do. In 1923, black rodeo star Bill Pickett, along with other black cowboys and cowgirls, performed feats of heroism and skill in *The Bull-Dogger*. *The Flaming Crisis* (1924) focused on a tough black newspaperman falsely accused of murder, fighting to prove his innocence. *The Flying Ace* (1926) spotlighted a daring black navigator who, in midair, rescues a black damsel in distress. In these films, black Americans saw themselves incorporated into the national pop mythology, and a

new set of archetypes emerged: heroic black protagonists (mainly men) of action. Whether cowboys, detectives, or weary army vets, many of these early characters were walking embodiments of black assertion and aggression, and of course, they gave lie to America's notions of a Negro's place.

Among the most interesting films were those which offered high-minded statements on the nature of black life in America or on the racial dynamics—divisions and tensions—within the black community.

Nowhere was a race theme more apparent than in *Scar of Shame* (1927). Produced by the Colored Players of Philadelphia, this slow-moving and melancholy film told the story of the ill-matched marriage between a young black pianist and a poor lower-class young black woman. Secretly ashamed of his wife, the young man keeps her hidden from his socially prominent middle-class mother. In a series of likably implausible plot maneuvers, the two part. He begins life anew and falls in love with another woman, only to meet up with his wife again. She still loves him, but knows she can never be his equal. Socially, although both are black, they are of different worlds. Despondent, the wife commits suicide and frees her husband to marry the other woman, his social equal. Melodramatic but effective, *Scar of Shame* was a surprisingly eloquent statement on the class and color caste system that existed within the black community.

OSCAR MICHEAUX: PIONEER SHOWMAN AUTEUR

No early independent African-American filmmaker was more important than the indefatigable producer/director Oscar Micheaux. A charismatic showman with a dash and flair he no doubt felt befitted a motion-picture director, Micheaux was dedicated to his own concept of black cinema (a heady mix of subliminal social messages and sheer pop entertainment), and perhaps also to the creation of his own personal legend.

Born in 1884, he had once been a Pullman car porter, then a farmer in South Dakota, and by 1915, also a door-to-door salesman of his first self-published novel, *The Homesteader*. Within a few years, he turned to film, his fervid enthusiasm for moviemaking eventually carrying him to Chicago and later New York. Through sheer drive coupled with a shrewd promotional sense, he was able to write, direct, and produce, by some accounts, thirty to forty-some films from 1918 to 1948.

Micheaux's features were similar to Hollywood's but technically inferior. Lighting and editing were often poor, and the acting could be dreadful—ranging from actors winging it to those grandstanding. Often a scene was shot in a single take. Since he was forced to shoot scenes so rapidly, he seldom had time (or money) to do retakes. Consequently, an actor might flub a line, then just pick up the pieces of his sentence and keep on going.

Oddly enough, Micheaux's limitations—the uncontrolled

performances and the lived-in look of some sets (sometimes he filmed in actual locations)—endowed his films with a strange realism. One half expects to hear Micheaux call "Cut" and to see the actors walk away from the camera or express their excitement over the fact that they're actually making a movie.

Intertwined in his film is the consciousness of race as a force in black life. Sometimes Micheaux took the typical Hollywood script and gave it a black slant. His *Underworld* (1937) was a gangster film: the recent grad of a good colored college in the South goes North, where he gets himself mixed up in Chicago's crime world. *Daughter of the Congo* (1930) was an African adventure story about a United States military officer bent on rescuing a young Negro girl captured by Arab slave hunters in a savage land.

On occasion, Micheaux focused exclusively on race as a subject, as in *Birthright* (1924), the story of a young black Harvard graduate who returns to his hometown in Tennessee bent on founding a colored school to "uplift the race." Naturally, he encounters opposition, some of which comes from his fellow blacks, who agree with white Southerners that education ruins a Negro. In its own corny and sly way, *Birthright* made a definite plea for black unity, while satirizing the old-style turncoats and toms. Micheaux liked this material so much that he remade the film in 1939.

Dazzled by Hollywood's star system, Micheaux also saw the significance of stars for his type of cinema. *The Brute* (1920) featured boxer Sam Langford with actress Evelyn Preer. His *Body and Soul* (1924) starred a strapping newcomer, Paul Robeson, as a shifty black minister. Micheaux dubbed his leading players black versions of white stars: thus Lorenzo Tucker became the "black Valentino"; Bee Freeman, the "sepia Mae West."

Within his star system, Micheaux gave his actresses vivid and important roles. Several of his films might well be classified as "women's pictures," dramas that focused on the tensions

and drives, the restless energies of independent, strong-willed heroines in conflict with men, with themselves, or with the world in which they lived. *God's Step Children* (ca. 1937), which told the tale of the Negress Naomi, who decides to cross the color line, was part woman's film, part race-theme movie, its heroine ultimately punished with death (like Dinah in *Underworld*), perhaps precisely because of her freewheeling independence. Micheaux's wife, actress Alice B. Russell, also worked closely with him behind the scenes on his production, perhaps helping him to inject a female perspective into some of his melodramas.

Micheaux clearly realized (and relished) the importance of promotion and publicity. He is said to have toured the country to publicize one film and at the same time seek financing for his next, often stepping out of cars and into meeting halls as if "he were God about to deliver a sermon." "Why, he was so impressive and so charming," said actor Lorenzo Tucker, "that he could talk the shirt off your back." On his tours, Micheaux approached white Southern theater managers and owners, often persuading them to show his black films at special matinee performances for black audiences or at special late shows for white audiences interested in black camp. Micheaux's shrewd promotional sense kept him in business, even after a major setback in 1928, when he went bankrupt and then had to reorganize.

Oscar Micheaux's greatest contribution is often viewed by some contemporary black audiences as his severest shortcoming. That his films frequently reflected the interests and values of the black bourgeoisie has long been held against him. Though his films did not center on the racial misery and decay of the ghetto, few race movies did. Instead, they tended to concentrate on the problems facing black "professional people."

Often enough, too, his favored leads were close to the white ideal: straight-haired, keen-featured, light-skinned. (The same was true of other race movies.) Micheaux was some-

times criticized by the black press for his color caste system. In an *Amsterdam News* review of Micheaux's *Daughter of the Congo*, black critic Theophilus Lewis complained: "The first offense of the new film is its persistent vaunting of interracial color fetishism. The scene is laid in a not so mythical republic in Africa. Half of the characters wear European clothes and are supposed to be civilized, while the other half wear their birthday suits and some feathers and are supposed to be savages. All the noble characters are high yellows; all the ignoble ones are black."

Lewis continued: "Even if the picture possessed no other defects, this artificial association of nobility with lightness and villainy with blackness would be enough to ruin it. It is based on a false assumption that has no connection with the realities of life."

Perhaps to best appreciate Micheaux's films, one must understand that he was moving as far as possible from mainstream cinema's jesters and servants. He wanted to give his audience something "to further the race, not hinder it." In doing so, Micheaux's films could also be controversial. His *Within Our Gates* (1920) had a lynching sequence which the Chicago Board of Movie Censors objected to. Today his films remain a fascinating comment on black social and political aspirations of the past.

The audience for black films grew rapidly (particularly between 1915 and 1923); eventually there were about 600 theaters on the race-movie circuit. But a number of basic problems plagued this burgeoning industry: financing, distribution, promotion. When talking movies came into vogue, many companies lacked the capital to keep up production and to acquire the new sound equipment. Micheaux, crafty as ever, was one of the few black directors who managed to make the transition from silent to sound cinema. In 1931, he released—with some fanfare—the first black talking film, *The Exile*, which had a splashy opening in Harlem that the black press was eager to publicize.

A headline in *The Pittsburgh Courier* proclaimed: "Oscar Micheaux's First Big Venture in Dramatic Talking Field Acclaimed in New York by Large Crowd—Cast Scores." The article reported:

> *The Exile*, billed as the first all-Negro talking picture by a picked cast of performers, telling a story of Negro life in an intimate way by a Negro author, got its first screening at the Lafayette Theatre, Saturday afternoon, and was greeted by more than an overflow audience that had waited more than six months to see just what appeal the picture had for a Metropolitan audience. In this picture, they got an eye full [sic], for *The Exile* carries everything that a modern picture should have to hold the interest. There is a nice plot, a love story as gripping as it possibly can be and the portrayal of Negro life in a city that no one but a Negro, who has travelled and lived in cities, could tell. Besides, there are those real actors, used for the first time on the screen, who do an excellent job before the strong light.

THE SOUND ERA: HOLLYWOOD GOES BLACK

Ironically, the sound era opened doors for African-American performers in Hollywood. The moment Al Jolson strutted in blackface to sing "Mammy" in *The Jazz Singer* (1927), American motion pictures underwent an extraordinary change. The sound medium required a new type of star, a new type of energy and style, indeed an entirely new kind of rhythm. Soon Hollywood turned its eye and ear to New York theater and nightclubs for performers who not only had faces but *voices*, too. Studio executives no doubt also spotted something else on the New York scene.

During the 1920s, amid the dazzle and rich creativity of the Harlem Renaissance, New York nightlife—the clubs, the speakeasies, the theaters—was invigorated by the style and presence of such Negro entertainers as Ethel Waters, Bill "Bojangles" Robinson, Florence Mills, Duke Ellington, and Josephine Baker, all of whom, quiet as it was kept, infused American popular culture with a new perspective, a new flash, a new kind of energy and *attitude*. The Negro entertainer

*Daniel Haynes and Nina Mae McKinney in **Hallelujah** (1929)*

was now becoming a very acceptable presence within the cultural mainstream, albeit in certain roles. This new acceptability was not lost on Hollywood. There were even rumors that the Negro voice recorded better than the white one. Almost immediately, too, some believed sound films could prove important to African-Americans.

In a 1928 *Pittsburgh Courier* feature titled "Talkies May Help Race Artists!" Floyd J. Calvin wrote about the possibilities and ironies talking cinema might offer black performers:

> A humorous story is told of how the "talkies" are playing havoc with the old actors. It is said that Farina [the child star of Hal Roach's silent "Our Gang" series] was tried out with the "talkies" with the expectation that he would use the broken English suitable to the characters he portrays in the silent drama. However, Farina was born in Boston and has had the best of tutors, so when he opened his mouth his English did credit to Fifth Avenue's most polite social circles. On the other hand, it is said when Adolphe Menjou, the evening clothes idol, was tried out in the "talkies" his English was so atrocious it was suggested that Farina be allowed to do his talking while Menjou acted, and Menjou be allowed to do Farina's talking while Farina acted. Such is the upset the "talkies" have caused in the cinema world.

In 1929, two major film studios, Fox and M-G-M, released two all-talking, all-singing colored motion pictures, *Hearts in Dixie* and *Hallelujah*. Here for the first time in Hollywood cinema, audiences saw real African-American performers in leading roles. Thus, by the very nature of their casts, each was a groundbreaker. Each was also an earnest attempt at providing some comment on African-American life and culture. Yet their results were mixed, primarily because both *Hearts in Dixie* and *Hallelujah* relied on familiar, at times soothing and comforting, black images.

Hearts in Dixie offered spirited music, some energetic dancing, some comedy, some sentimentality, and a portrait of docile, childlike backwoods Southern Negroes. In its favorable review, *The New York Times* commented: "And as the evidently pleasing throngs who had hitherto worshiped at the shrine of jazz slowly issued from the theatre, one heard compliments for the picture and then somebody humming 'Massa's in the Cold, Cold Ground.'" Of course, a chorus of "Massa's in the Cold, Cold Ground" was hardly an image that would give its audience any pause to think about the place of the Negro in American life.

In a cast of then unknowns that included Clarence Muse, Mildred Washington, Eugene Jackson, and Gertrude Howard, one performer stood out: a skinny, lanky, limber roustabout named Stepin Fetchit. Earlier Fetchit had cracked the Hollywood system to appear in stereotyped roles in such films as *In Old Kentucky* (1927) and *The Ghost Talks* (1929). Here in this black setting, where he related to other black characters and presented but one image in a series of images, Fetchit's lazy coon character was not as disturbing as it would later be

***Stepin Fetchit in* The Kansan (1943)**

in films of the 1930s, when Fetchit had to perform relentlessly demeaning antics for the benefit of his white co-stars. His performance in *Hearts in Dixie* may well be the very one that audiences today can watch to understand his impact and the nature of his talent and why a black critic like James Weldon Johnson called Fetchit "a pretty good clown."

Critic Robert Benchley also found Fetchit an impressive one-of-a-kind performer in the new talking films. In the April 1929 issue of the National Urban League publication *Opportunity*, Benchley commented on "the amazing personality of Stepin Fetchit." He wrote: "I see no reason for hesitating in saying that he is the best actor that the talking movies have produced. His voice, his manner, his timing, everything that he does, is as near to perfection as one could hope to get in an essentially phony medium such as this. You forget that you are listening to a synchronized sound-track which winds its way along the side of a photographic film." Benchley added: "When Stepin Fetchit speaks, you are there beside him, one of the great comedians of the screen."

Benchley also commented on the new medium and the Negro voice:

> With the opening of *Hearts in Dixie*, however, the future of the talking-movie has taken on a rosier hue. Voices can be found which will register perfectly. Personalities can be found which are ideal for this medium. It may be that the talking-movies must be participated in exclusively by Negroes, but, if so, then so be it.

In the Negro the sound-picture has found its ideal protagonist. There is a quality in the Negro voice, an ease in its delivery and a sense of timing in reading the lines, which make it the ideal medium for the talking-picture. What white actors are going to do to compete with it is their business. So long as there are enough Negroes to make pictures, and enough good stories for them to act in, the future of the talking-picture is assured . . . The fact remains, however, that many people will remember *Hearts in Dixie* as the first talking-picture in which the characters seemed really to talk, and will remember its Negro cast as the first real actors they ever saw in talking-pictures.

Benchley's high hopes for the future of the talking picture and the Negro actor were not fulfilled. Yet, perhaps just as the studio had hoped, a new kind of energy and sound had indeed made its way to the screen.

The same was true of King Vidor's *Hallelujah.* In his autobiography, *A Tree Is a Tree,* Vidor wrote: "For several years I had nurtured a secret hope. I wanted to make a film about Negroes, using only Negroes in the cast. The sincerity and fervor of their religious expression intrigued me, as did the honest simplicity of their sexual drives." But the studio executives always said no until, Vidor said, "with sound pictures I had a new argument." Even at that, M-G-M balked that such a film would never be shown in white Southern theaters. Vidor finally got to make the movie by investing his salary in it.

Moody, poetic, lyrical, moving, and beautifully shot on location in the swamps and forests of Tennessee and Arkansas, *Hallelujah* sensitively looked at the plight of a weak field laborer, Zeke, lured away from his family and the church by the charms of a spicy young woman of, shall we say, "easy virtue." Vidor's characters were again gentle, childlike, lost figures, but with a tragic dimension. The director fully valued the talents of his cast, which he showcased brilliantly. Daniel Haynes, with his Robesonesque voice and stance, was a moving Zeke. Blues singer Victoria Spivey played the sweet-girl-back-home, Missy Rose. Also in the cast were Fannie Belle de Knight and William Fountaine.

But the center of *Hallelujah* was Nina Mae McKinney's performance—playful, energetic, sexy, girlish—as the likably naughty, high-strung strumpet Chick, who leads the hero astray. McKinney won accolades from the critics, and both Vidor and M-G-M producer Irving Thalberg. It looked as if she was well on her way to becoming American cinema's first black leading lady. But while Hollywood might experiment with its idea of a black slice-of-life picture, the industry still was not ready for a black love goddess.

McKinney endured a fate that such talented black female stars as Dorothy Dandridge and Lonette McKee would later experience: after one dazzling performance (Dandridge in *Carmen Jones* in 1954; McKee in *Sparkle* in 1976), few, if any, important follow-up roles materialized. McKinney was left

floundering. In 1931, she played a small but interesting role in *Safe in Hell,* then appeared at clubs and cabarets in Europe (where she was called the "black Garbo"), starred opposite Paul Robeson in the British film *Sanders of the River* (1935), and, once back in the States, played glamour-girl leads in such race movies as *The Gang Smashers* (1938), *The Devil's Daughter* (1939), and *Straight to Heaven* (1939). In 1949, she returned to Hollywood for a supporting role in her last important film, *Pinky.* But her full potential was left untapped.

When neither *Hallelujah* nor *Hearts in Dixie* proved a box-office success, Hollywood backed away from the black movie, considering it box-office poison. The idea that there might be an African-American audience out there for whom such a film could be developed and pitched never dawned on Hollywood. Not until seven years later—when Warner Brothers released *The Green Pastures*—would Hollywood take a chance on another black film.

Still, *Hearts in Dixie,* and particularly *Hallelujah,* received wide black and white press coverage, debating their pros and cons. In September 1929, a headline in New York's *Amsterdam News* announced: "Dr. W.E.B. Du Bois Praises *Hallelujah.*" It referred to Du Bois's comments on the film in the October 1929 issue of the NAACP's magazine *Crisis.*

"It is the sense of real life without the exaggerated farce and horseplay," wrote Du Bois, "which most managers regard as inseparable from Negro character, that marks *Hallelujah* as epoch-making. It goes without saying that the characters do their parts superbly. And why not? King Vidor had choice of a neglected field overflowing with undeveloped talent. The fine, sensitive face and intelligent acting of Daniel Haynes were notable, the slim grace of Miss McKinney, the restraint of Miss Spivey, and the playing of Harry Gray and Mrs. De Knight were excellent. Even the kids danced as country boys would and not as city sophisticates. The music was lovely and while I would have preferred more spirituals instead of the theme-song, yet the world is not as crazy about Negro talk songs as I am. Everybody should see *Hallelujah.*"

And so, in 1929, at the close of one era and the start of another, the Negro entertainer had indeed added a special spark and a new dimension to American movies in general and to the new talking motion picture in particular. That same year Ethel Waters performed "Am I Blue?" and "Birmingham Bertha" in *On with the Show.* Bessie Smith also made her one and only movie appearance in the short film *St. Louis Blues* (1929), while Duke Ellington and his orchestra and a lovely unknown named Fredi Washington appeared in *Black and Tan* (1929).

THE DEPRESSION ERA: HOLLYWOOD'S COMIC SERVANTS

During the next decade—the years of the Great Depression—even more African-American actors and actresses

found opportunities in Hollywood cinema. Working side by side with such icons as Gable, Harlow, Hepburn, Dietrich, Fonda, W. C. Fields, and Mae West, and under the direction of such filmmakers as John Ford, George Stevens, George Cukor, and Victor Fleming, African-Americans, more often than not, found themselves cast in shamelessly stereotyped roles. Today, when one thinks of the typical lazy, bug-eyed, black movie stereotype, most likely it is an image from 1930s Hollywood.

Usually, they played dizzy comic servants who performed a funny antic or "hilarious" piece of dialogue and then disappeared from the film. Or the servants proved themselves ever loyal standbys, seemingly existing with no other purpose in life than to please or reassure their white employers.

During this economically and politically troubled era, the Negro servants were used to provide America with a comforting set of fantasies: often their presence suggested that nothing was ever too bad if everyone, black and white, somehow stuck together (and, naturally, never forgot his or her place); or the notion that, in the worst of times, if the lowly

Negro could keep up his or her spirits, well, then, why couldn't *everyone* else? Hollywood films did not seek to establish a cultural background/context for their black characters, to say something about their lives away from their white bosses or to comment on basic inequities in the American system. In mainstream cinema, everything just seemed honky-dory.

Yet despite such rigidly limited and typed roles, a number of black performers came up with highly individualized performances and developed trademark screen personas. The trick for the Negro performer of the 1930s and in the many decades to follow was not simply to play a role (as written) but, rather, to play against it: to pump up tired, clichéd, distorted, and demeaning parts with some much needed energy, wit, insight, style, and personal idiosyncrasies.

In the early Depression years, Stepin Fetchit was Hollywood's most important black performer. In such movies as *David Harum* (1934), *Judge Priest* (1934), and *Stand Up and Cheer* (1934), he continued to play the dense lackey. Curiously, like certain other black performers who followed him, Fetchit sometimes appeared to operate in his own world,

Hattie McDaniel and Jeanne Crain in **Margie** *(1946)*

with an ironic detachment from the degrading proceedings he participated in. He also performed at his own idiosyncratic rhythm, refusing ever to be rushed through a scene with a co-star and managing, ironically, to command screen time—*and* audience attention. When he was on screen, it was impossible to watch anyone else.

During Fetchit's early period, the black press covered his activities. In 1933, after Fetchit had resolved problems with his studio, Fox, Norfolk's *Journal and Guide* enthusiastically reported on the comic's new contract: "That famous lazy clown, of the stage and screen, Stepin Fetchit, will have his shuffling bones and slowest drawl reflected from America's silver screen again . . . Fox has re-signed Stepin Fetchit. The colored performer who had such a promising movie career will be given another chance."

In time, though, Fetchit's characters came to represent the worst type of black stereotype: the black man as the lazy, bewildered, stammering, shuffling, dimwitted no-account. In a film like *Judge Priest*, he was barely intelligible, scratched his head in an apelike fashion, and followed white co-star Will Rogers around like an adored pet. Today his great talents look shockingly misused. By the end of the decade, the actor who opened the door for blacks in Hollywood left the film capital and drifted into obscurity.

But other actors and actresses made their mark in the 1930s and early 1940s. In such features as *The Little Colonel* and *The Littlest Rebel* (both 1935), Bill "Bojangles" Robinson played the friendly, cheery tom figure to Shirley Temple's pint-sized heroines. When he had to speak, Bojangles could be downright embarrassing; sometimes he sounded as if he were reading from a primer. And often one wants to hear him voice some discontent about these ideal and romanticized worlds in which his characters function. But when called upon to dance—to teach little Shirley how to glide up the staircase in *The Little Colonel*—Bojangles was a marvel: all enthusiasm,

all unabashed joy, all smooth and polished perfection; a dancing presence unlike any other in the movies. For an era in need of some hopeful sign of endurance and coherence, Bojangles emerged as an optimistic icon, a symbol of sturdy unflappability.

Others also impressed audiences. With his gravelly cement mixer of a voice, Eddie "Rochester" Anderson was a plucky, sturdy, serenely confident "little guy," the clever manipulative servant in his later movies of the 1940s with Jack Benny, whom he was often able to outwit and outmaneuver.

In films such as *Alice Adams* (1935), *China Seas* (1935), and *The Mad Miss Manton* (1938), Hattie McDaniel (billed as Hattie McDaniels in the early years of her career) played amazingly self-assured and aggressive full-bodied mammies. Her voice was a powerful sonic boom of an instrument that she used skillfully to lace her lines with a perceptible hostility. Sometimes McDaniel seemed uptight or edgy, as if she *just did not want to be bothered* with the white folks she deigned to work for; of course, the films couldn't explain her mood. But audiences merely had to take one look at McDaniel to realize that here was a woman born to give, not take, orders.

The mammies played by Louise Beavers were more agreeable, less edgy. Beavers was able to impart a seemingly genuine and heartfelt sincerity and optimism into her cheap roles. The diminutive Butterfly McQueen, with her distinctive high-pitched voice, was a scatterbrained imp, often appearing, like Fetchit, to be performing in a different universe from the other characters in her films. Actors like Mantan Moreland and Willie Best played baffled and baffling coon servants, perfecting their timing and pacing, their double takes and eye pops, to the point where they were usually able to steal scenes like crazy.

No one in his right mind could ever claim that the roles these performers played were anything other than flat-out

W. C. Fields and Eddie "Rochester" Anderson in **You Can't Cheat an Honest Man** *(1939)*

Eddie "Rochester" Anderson

deplorable. Yet no one can deny that the actors and actresses were significant talents.

During this time, the black press was often excited by the presence of black performers in Hollywood cinema. In 1934, *The Pittsburgh Courier* carried an article with the headline "Mayor of Harlem Gets Key to Hollywood; Is Feature of New Flicker." The subhead announced: "Bill (Bojangles) Robinson and Hattie McDaniels in Shirley Temple Film—*Courier* Reporter Gets Exclusive Interview."

The article conveyed the black press's enthusiasm:

Flickering in the spotlight of Filmdom's capital is the world's greatest tap dancer, Bill (Bojangles) Robinson, debonair "Mayor of Harlem."

He is here in response to Fox Film's chief, Winfield Sheehan, who telephoned Bill in New York City the other day, asking if he would like a principal role in Shirley Temple's current cinema, *The Little Colonel*. The contract was agreed upon by long distance telephone from Hollywood to Harlem.

The article also expressed the belief that Robinson's

best work will be reeled in *The Little Colonel*, and you can believe me when I say that he and Hattie McDaniels, the buxom, ebony-hued Kate Smith, are a riot in this picture. I heard them rehearsing at the studio, and just a little line of their dialogue convulsed me as it did themselves. Just expect to hold your sides when you see the film. Bill and Hattie have trouped together on the Orpheum Circuit years ago, so this team's screen reunion will naturally top any performance that has ever been billed.

During this era, there were some exceptions to the general run of servant figures. Before working in Hollywood, Paul Robeson gave a forceful dramatic performance (that *Newsweek* called "brilliant") in the independently produced version of Eugene O'Neill's *Emperor Jones* (1933). Once Robeson arrived in the film capital, he played the lazy good-for-nothing Joe in *Show Boat* (1936). Yet Robeson's presence and per-

sonal bearing, his basic projection of strength and power (there was absolutely nothing servile about him), exposed the hollow mechanics of the plot. When he sang "Ol' Man River," he lifted the film on his massive shoulders and injected into this song the suggestion of black exploitation and oppression. It remains a classic sequence in the history of the American musical. Robeson also worked abroad in such films as *Song of Freedom* (1936) and *Proud Valley* (1940), in which he hoped to escape stereotyped roles.

Another exception was the 1934 version of *Imitation of Life*. Based on the novel by Fannie Hurst, it told the story of two women—one, Delilah, black (Louise Beavers); the other, Miss Bea, white (Claudette Colbert); each without a husband and each with a young daughter to raise—who meet by chance. The two women live together and come to great financial prosperity with the black woman's pancake recipe, which has been passed down in her family. The white woman markets a mix based on it, which becomes a phenomenal national success.

At one point, she offers Delilah a 20 percent interest in the budding company. How kind of the white woman, particularly since without the black woman there would have been no company at all! But Delilah indicates she does not want money or a home of her own. Her great aim in life is to remain (seemingly in servitude) by her white friend's side. In one haunting sequence, the two women—by now the best of friends and still living together once they have struck it rich—retire for the evening. The white woman goes upstairs. The black woman descends to the basement level.

Imitation of Life touched on the idea of white exploitation of the black woman, but the film steered clear of any real examination of such a theme. The film is now best remembered for another subject it raised, then backed away from: the story of the black woman's light-skinned daughter, Peola (Fredi Washington), who, in rebellion against her mother's submissiveness, decides to cross the color line and pass for white. The film's subtext was that of a black woman challenging America's ideas on race and setting out for the opportunities otherwise denied her.

No other Hollywood film of the era so poignantly affected or perhaps so unknowingly hit a nerve within the African-American community. Debates sprang up in the black press, which immediately grasped *Imitation of Life*'s significance. In the magazine *Opportunity*, black critic Sterling Brown wrote his famous essay "*Imitation of Life*: Once a Pancake," in which he criticized the stereotyped images, yet also stated that the movie "has its moments of truth to American life."

But few took issue with the actresses Louise Beavers and Fredi Washington, who had a chance to play the only significant dramatic roles then offered to black women in Hollywood. In its article "Louise Beavers Secured Film Role Through

Louise Beavers in **Imitation of Life (1934)**

Luck," the black newspaper *The Chicago Defender* reported: "Miss Beavers' role is second in importance only to that of the star, and gives her opportunities said to be exceptional."

In a *Pittsburgh Courier* article (that was run in other black newspapers as well) titled "Fredi Washington Strikes New Note in Hollywood Film," writer Fay M. Jackson wrote that, in *Imitation of Life*,

Fredi Washington, New York dancer-actress, utters a cry, "I want the same things other people enjoy," that found an echo in the hearts of twelve million Black folk throughout the United States and probably has echoed since their so-called emancipation from

chattel slavery. Actress though she be, Fredi Washington expresses the desire for freedom and equal justice in this picture that is more convincing than any mere performer could have voiced . . . Credit Fannie Hurst (or some colored informant) for conceiving *Imitations* [sic] *of Life*, John Stahl for directing it sympathetically, Fredi Washington, against heavy odds, for presenting the substance of the opus in a manner that is intelligent and convincingly true to life.

Imitation of Life remains a fascinating film. In 1959, a remake appeared (minus the pancake recipe) with Lana Turner, Juanita Moore (in an Oscar-nominated Best Supporting Actress per-

Fredi Washington

formance as the black servant figure), and white actress Susan Kohner as the daughter.

In 1936, Hollywood also released the all-black *The Green Pastures*. Based on a successful Broadway play by white writer Marc Connelly, it was a fantasy centering on an all-black heaven with "black versions" of biblical stories. Again the image of the Negro was that of the non-threatening, childlike naïf, now endowed with a certain homespun wisdom. Again gifted black actors such as Eddie Anderson (as Noah), Edna Mae Harris, Ernest Whitman, George Reed, Frank Wilson, and, most impressively, Rex Ingram (as the wise and humane heavenly host De Lawd) brought conviction to these parts.

The 1930s closed with a film that in many respects marked the end of the old-style full-blown servant figures: David O. Selznick's *Gone With the Wind*. Watching this romantic Civil War epic, one would never know the real issues of the War Between the States. Its focal point is the topsy-turvy relationship of Southern belle Scarlett O'Hara and Rhett Butler. Slavery is depicted as some sort of benign state. None of the principal black characters—Mammy, Prissy, Pork, Uncle Peter, Big Sam—appears to have any thought whatsoever of rebelling or, heaven forbid, of seeking freedom. Indeed, Mammy, as played by the ever resourceful Hattie McDaniel, seems to hold the Big House intact throughout the War.

Yet here McDaniel's edge is on prominent display. As the one character aware of Scarlett O'Hara's moves and maneuvers, Mammy rarely hesitates to speak up or, if necessary,

threaten her mistress. So thought out, confident, and vivid a characterization does McDaniel create that one wonders what becomes of Mammy when the cameras are not around: Exactly what does she do when she rips the bandanna from her head and leaves Scarlett's side? Where does Mammy live? Does she go out to the slave quarters at night? Does she have a room in the Big House? What is the nature of her relationships with the other servants, Pork and Prissy?

Gone With the Wind, however, has no interest in telling us about Mammy's other life (just as a film like *Driving Miss Daisy*, which came fifty years later, has no interest in revealing much about the life of its black chauffeur, Hoke, apart from the white woman he serves). For her performance in *Gone With the Wind* (1939), Hattie McDaniel became the first African-American performer to win the Academy Award—as Best Supporting Actress.

RACE MOVIES: THE 1930S AND 1940S

During the 1930s and 1940s, race-movie producers still struggled to pull together funds to finance films. Oscar Micheaux directed and produced until the release of his last film, *The Betrayal*, in 1948.

Another important African-American filmmaker of the period was Spencer Williams, who ironically is now best remembered for his role as the cigar-chomping Andy on the television series of the 1950s *Amos 'n' Andy*. Williams, however, was a unique director/writer/actor, who directed such personal "folk dramas" as *The Blood of Jesus* (1946) and *Go Down, Death* (1944), in which he examined aspects of the African-American religious experience, its imagery, symbols, and obsessions.

Other Williams-directed films included *Dirty Gertie from Harlem U.S.A.* (1946, a reworking of Somerset Maugham's *Rain*), the 1947 *Juke Joint* (which captures and evokes the rhythms and tones of old-style ethnic theater), *Jivin' in Be-Bop* (1946), *Marching On!* (1943), and *Beale Street Mama* (1947). He also wrote scripts for other films and acted in his own films as well as in other race movies.

Among the other African-American filmmakers of this era were George Randol and Ralph Cooper. In Los Angeles, they formed a production company to produce the gangster film *Dark Manhattan* (1937), which Cooper not only starred in but wrote as well. It premiered at the Tivoli Theatre in Los Angeles. In his autobiography, *Amateur Night at the Apollo*, Cooper recalled that the film was also

a huge hit in Harlem. I got a big kick out of hearing that when the movie was screened at the Apollo, it broke all attendance records back in my home theatre. [Robert] Schiffman played the movie at the Apollo and the Harlem Opera House at the same time. People naturally wanted to see it at the Apollo even though it cost more, because they got to see the stage show along with

Hattie McDaniel and Vivien Leigh in **Gone With the Wind**
(1939)

the film. So he oversold every performance at the Apollo, and when the seats were filled, he sent the extra ticket holders down to the Harlem Opera House. That's how they broke the all-time attendance record at the Apollo—by selling twice as many tickets as there were seats. Despite the fact that the contract called for the Apollo only and it was a flat buy not a percentage, what nobody knew was that Schiffman had only one print of the film. So as one reel ended at the Apollo, it was rewound by Doll Thomas, the projectionist, and rushed down to the Harlem Opera House, where it was played; and as soon as the second reel was screened at the Opera House, it had to be rewound again and rushed back to the Apollo in time for the second screening there.

Here we see the kind of excitement certain race movies engendered within the black audience. *Dark Manhattan* also drew some attention from the mainstream press, which generally did not review race films. The reviewer for *Variety* wrote:

All colored-cast meller framed around the Harlem numbers racket operation will get by in Negro houses chiefly because of the novelty it embodies for such audiences in that no white person is lensed in the footage. Following its premiere in Harlem, it has already been booked into pretty good colored theatres in 16 key towns around the country.

Produced in Hollywood, film is best technically ever made with complete colored cast. Unfortunately, scripting and acting don't part the mechanical manufacture, and among the players there are few that really mean meat on a marquee. Ralph Cooper, its star, is the stand-out.

Later Cooper joined Million Dollar Pictures with the white backers Harry and Leo Popkin. He was also the man behind the screen debut of a very pretty but plump ingenue named Lena Horne, who, before working in Hollywood, appeared in the 1938 race movie *The Duke Is Tops.* In her autobiography, *Lena,* Horne spoke of her experiences on the film, which capture some of the frantic energy and problems inherent in race-movie productions:

I received a call from Harold Gumm, who was an agent in New York [she wrote]. He had remembered me from my days at the Cotton Club and now he was rounding up talent for a little quickie Negro musical that was about to be shot in Hollywood. It was called *The Duke Is Tops*, starring Ralph Cooper, who had been an emcee at the Apollo Theatre. It was being produced by some shoestring independents, the Popkin Brothers, and they wanted me for a part. The shooting schedule was only ten days.

Horne also remembered money problems. "The producers apparently had not completed their financing before starting up and they were paying off in promises of what we would make later, when the picture went into release."

Regardless, according to Ralph Cooper, "The cast, the shoot, and the finished product were all great. I was certain it would appeal to a broad audience of African-Americans and I was right. The picture enjoyed sensational box office. The billing read 'Ralph Cooper in *The Duke Is Tops*, with Lena Horne.'"

In his autobiography, Cooper also recalled:

Then a funny thing happened. After we wrapped, Lena had been engaged to perform a vocal in an MGM musical that became an enormous hit. There were a total of nine hundred black theatres in the U.S. then, and our film played in about six hundred of them (at least three hundred were owned by competitors). There were, at the same time, some thirty-five thousand movie houses catering to white audiences in the U.S. Once that huge audience saw Lena in the MGM musical, she became a very hot Hollywood property. *The Duke Is Tops* was reissued with a change of title and new billing: "Lena Horne in *The Bronze Venus* with Ralph Cooper." There were no credits on the poster saying that Ralph Cooper wrote and directed the picture.

Other black filmmakers of the time included Eddie Green and William Alexander, who produced *Souls of Sin* (1949) and *The Fight Never Ends* (1947) with Joe Louis, Ruby Dee, and William Greaves. Years later Alexander produced the Hollywood film *The Klansman*, with Richard Burton, Lee Marvin, and Lola Falana. Actor Greaves went on to an impressive career as the director of such documentaries as *Still a Brother: Inside the Negro Middle Class* (1968) and *From These Roots* (1974), a *tour de force* look at figures of the Harlem Renaissance.

Perhaps the most important shift in the late 1930s/1940s was the goal of later race-movie producers, most of whom were white, to make slick and glossy products that resembled typical Hollywood fare: black Westerns, musicals, mysteries, gangster sagas, melodramas, and crime stories. Concentrating more on entertainment unencumbered by weighty messages about race, the new features nonetheless—simply because of their black casts—did not entirely leave the race issue behind. Thus the new stars, whether it was Herbert Jeffrey (also known as singer Herb Jeffries) as a spiffy cowboy immaculately dressed in tight riding clothes and fancy silver spurs and guns in *The Bronze Buckaroo* (1938) or later such well-scrubbed figures as William Greaves and Sheila Guyse in *Miracle in Harlem* (1948) or *Sepia Cinderella* (1947), remained indelible black middle-class heroes and heroines, still promoted as an ideal for the black masses. In the postwar era, they looked like sparkling symbols of a new segment of black America, now ready to integrate into the dominant mainstream culture.

But race movies were not free of stereotypes. While lighter blacks continued to play the leads, darker performers were sometimes relegated to supporting roles as comic figures, not too different from those in Hollywood films.

Pepped up and faster-moving, escapist and high-spirited, the 1930s/1940s films also often featured musical stars or introduced new personalities. Besides Lena Horne, Dorothy Dandridge was another performer who, before becoming a Hollywood star in such films as *Bright Road* (1953), *Carmen Jones* (1954), and *Porgy and Bess* (1959), proved a lovely and fresh presence in such race movies as *Four Shall Die* (1940) and *Ebony Parade* (1947). The Mills Brothers, Nat "King" Cole, Juano Hernandez, Robert Earl Jones (the father of James Earl Jones), and jazz vocalist Helen Humes all performed for the later race-movie cameras.

A number of other black Hollywood performers, in need of a break and a breath of fresh air away from the major studios, worked in race movies in which they sometimes had a chance for a different type of role. Clarence Muse, Nina Mae McKinney, Mantan Moreland, Bill "Bojangles" Robinson, and Louise Beavers were launched as genuine stars in race movies with roles tailor-made for them.

Moreland, best known for his befuddled, scared-of-ghosts chauffeur character Birmingham Brown in the Charlie Chan series, starred in all-colored features that openly celebrated his wide-eyed manic energy: he had top billing in such movies as *Come On, Cowboy!* (1948) and *She's Too Mean for Me* (1948). *Mantan Messes Up* and *Mantan Runs for Mayor* (both 1946) were star vehicles developed around him. His success in the race-movie market indicates that African-American audiences were willing to accept Moreland in an all-black cultural context in which his daffy coon antics were viewed, not as some definitive statement on the black experience; instead, he was simply an oddball funnyman in a world full of other black images. The same held true for Stepin Fetchit, who, after his Hollywood heyday, appeared in such race movies as *Miracle in Harlem* (1948) and *Big Timers* (1945), playing the same type of dimwitted character. But no one seemed to mind.

The later race movies also made a place for a figure Hollywood seemed to have no use for at all: the unabashed, unchangeable, raunchy or rowdy "chitlin circuit" ethnic star who wasn't about to clean up his or her act (to tone down cultural differences or smooth out rough ethnic edges) to please a large white audience. Thus Jackie "Moms" Mabley, Dusty "Open the Door, Richard" Fletcher, Dewey "Pigmeat" Markham, and the great rhythm-and-blues star Louis Jordan did star spins in such films as *Killer Diller* (1948), *Boarding House Blues* (1948), *Fight That Ghost* (1946), and *Look-Out Sister* (1946).

HOLLYWOOD'S WAR YEARS

Throughout the 1940s, Hollywood images were affected by new attitudes and outlooks—in both white and black America—brought on by the Second World War. When black GIs marched off to fight, they did so in openly segregated units. When they returned home, they came face to face with the undeniable realization that, while they had defended the freedom of others abroad, they were without full rights in their own country—the land of the free and home of the brave. Within the African-American community, such leaders as A. Philip Randolph and Adam Clayton Powell, Jr.,

spoke out against discrimination and bigotry. In 1943, race riots broke out in Beaumont, Texas, Detroit, and Harlem.

In the early 1940s, Walter White, the Executive Secretary of the NAACP, traveled to Hollywood and, with the help of Wendell Willkie (a special counsel to the NAACP and also a 20th Century–Fox board member), spoke to industry leaders about new roles for Negroes in films. Long critical of Hollywood's black images, he urged that the Negro be presented as a normal human being.

White also took an interest in the career of screen newcomer Lena Horne, convinced that she could do much to alter the image of African-American women in movies. Horne became the first black woman to be fully glamorized and publicized by her studio, M-G-M. She never played maids. But she did not become a full-fledged dramatic star either. Usually, Horne, as well as pianist Hazel Scott, who also worked in Hollywood in the 1940s, appeared in nightclub sequences of films starring whites. On some occasions, when it was thought Horne's sequences might offend white Southern audiences, her scenes were simply clipped.

*Mantan Moreland and Frankie Darro in **Irish Luck** (1939)*

Cabin in the Sky (1943)

Still, in the early 1940s, Hollywood occasionally offered more sympathetic portraits of black characters in such films as *Sahara*, *Bataan*, *The Ox-Bow Incident* (all 1943), and John Huston's *In This Our Life* (1942). In the last, a sensitive, intelligent young black man (played by Ernest Anderson) is unjustly accused of a hit-and-run accident. In a heartfelt sequence, Hattie McDaniel, who played his troubled mother, expressed concern for her son and also revealed her range as an actress.

In 1943, Hollywood released two all-black musicals, *Cabin in the Sky* and *Stormy Weather*. Lena Horne starred in both. Based on the Broadway play and directed by Vincente Minnelli, *Cabin in the Sky* was yet another fantasy: this time around, an all black heaven and all black hell fight for the soul of aimless, harmless Little Joe Jackson, skillfully played by Eddie "Rochester" Anderson. His loyal, religious wife, Petunia (Ethel Waters), is heaven's greatest asset. His sexy lady friend, Georgia Brown (Horne), is his greatest temptation. Completely removed from then contemporary issues of Negro life, *Cabin in the Sky* nonetheless softened the old-style stereotypes and was invigorated by the first-rate performances of its all-star cast: Rex Ingram, Mantan Moreland, Butterfly McQueen, Oscar Polk, John "Bubbles" Sublett, Ford L. Washington (who with Sublett comprised the team Buck and Bubbles), Duke Ellington, Louis Armstrong, and Kenneth Spencer.

Short on plot, *Stormy Weather* also boasted an array of dazzling legendary performers: Bill "Bojangles" Robinson, Lena Horne, Fats Waller (performing "Ain't Misbehavin'"), Cab Calloway, Ada Brown, Flournoy Miller and Johnny Lee, Katherine Dunham and her dance company, Nicodemus, and Dooley Wilson (who played Sam in *Casablanca*). In a memorable sequence, Horne, looking melancholic and forlorn, stood by a window as she sang the title song, which afterward became forever associated with her. No doubt, most spectacular was the kinetic, show-stopping sequence performed by two of

the screen's greatest and perhaps most underrated dancers, the incomparable Nicholas Brothers, who brought *Stormy Weather* to an implausibly exhilarating climax. It is simply one of the screen's most spectacular dance sequences.

As with previous black Hollywood films, neither *Stormy Weather* nor *Cabin in the Sky* was a box-office hit. Yet today both films have acquired classic status: they remain invaluable cultural documents without which we might not have preserved on film a group of extraordinary, legendary black stars at the height of their creative powers.

THE POSTWAR ERA: NEW IMAGES, NEW STARS

Much of this changed, indeed came to an end, at the close of the 1940s. By then, race movies were on their last legs, victims of a changing market. During the postwar era, the major studios showed budding interest in blacks as vehicles for the metaphor of American justice. In 1949, Hollywood released four groundbreaking problem pictures: *Home of the Brave*, *Pinky*, *Lost Boundaries*, and *Intruder in the Dust*, each of which examined the race question.

Home of the Brave was promoted as "The First Motion Picture of Its Kind: Here is Hollywood's greatest blow at racial hatred." It starred newcomer James Edwards as a black soldier who, during a mission to fight for his country, suffers an emotional breakdown when he finds himself a victim of racism within his military unit.

In *Pinky*, a young light-skinned black woman (played by white actress Jeanne Crain), having endured the pain and indignity of bigotry in the South, considers returning to the North, where she will live as a free *white* woman. Playing the young woman's grandmother was that powerhouse Ethel Waters, who won an Academy Award nomination for Best Supporting Actress.

Lost Boundaries, based on a true story, explored the plight

Richard Wright in* Native Son *(1950)

Juano Hernandez in* Intruder in the Dust *(1949)

of a light-skinned black family living as whites in a small New England town. When their "dark" secret is revealed, they find themselves rejected by their friends and community.

And the adaptation of William Faulkner's novel *Intruder in the Dust* focused on a defiantly proud and stubborn black man, Lucas Beauchamp (played magnificently by the great Juano Hernandez), wrongly accused of having killed a white Southern neighbor.

In all these films, the idea of racial conflict and racism stood front and center. Here, too, the African-American character was no longer singing and dancing in an isolated, insulated world. Instead, he or she was a troubled, bruised, and brooding figure: a postwar social symbol.

Although the films were not without compromises, they managed nonetheless, as Ralph Ellison wrote in his essay "The Shadow and the Act," to get at deep centers of American emotion. "Dealing with matters which, over the years, have been slowly charging up with guilt," Ellison wrote, "they all display a vitality which escapes their slickest devices." Ellison also wrote that

the temptation toward self-congratulation which comes from seeing these films and sharing in their emotional release is apt to blind us to the true nature of what is unfolding—or failing to unfold—before our eyes. As an antidote to the sentimentality of these films, I suggest that they be seen in predominantly Negro audiences. For here, when the action goes phony, one will hear derisive laughter, not sobs . . . *Intruder in the Dust* is the only film that could be shown in Harlem without arousing unintended laughter. For it's the only one of the four in which Negroes can make complete identification with their screen image. Interestingly, the factors that make this identification possible lie in its depiction not of racial but of human quality.

The old race movies could not compete with the technically well-made Hollywood products. But more significantly, the African-American audience now had an altered vision of itself. During the rise of the civil rights movement, the audience sought a different kind of movie product, often considering the racially hermetically sealed worlds of the race movies passé.

In the fifties, audiences responded to such dramatic black stars as Dorothy Dandridge and Sidney Poitier in major Hollywood films. In the films *Carmen Jones* and *Porgy and Bess*, Dandridge's haughty glamour and tragic grandeur turned her into an authentic new-style cultural icon for black America. At the same time, the audience seemed to prefer such films

Dorothy Dandridge

as *No Way Out* (1950), *Edge of the City* (1957), and *The Defiant Ones* (1958), which promoted the theme of racial integration (and sometimes cultural assimilation) and which also, despite serious flaws or compromises, touched on conflicts between black and white. The latter was something race movies had rarely done. So they faded away.

THE NEW INDEPENDENTS

Of course, in subsequent decades African-American images, performers, and films would undergo yet other significant changes. During the 1960s, Sidney Poitier emerged as a major figure in Hollywood: the only black actor to work consistently in leading dramatic roles in American films. In 1963, he won the Academy Award as Best Actor, for *Lilies of the Field*.

But by the 1970s, the Poitier screen hero was replaced by a new set of gritty, rebellious, outspoken characters: Sweetback, Shaft, and Super Fly, all heroes in films created by such African-American filmmakers as Melvin Van Peebles, Gordon Parks, Sr., and Gordon Parks, Jr. Often the new films, many of which were male fantasies, seemed to be open declarations of war between black and white. The films picked up on the political energies and tensions within the African-American community of the late 1960s and early 1970s.

In the 1970s, other black directors and writers (such as Bill Gunn, Michael Schultz, Stan Lathan, Maya Angelou, Richard Wesley, Hugh Robertson, Lonne Elder III) worked in Hollywood. Also, independent black filmmakers such as William Greaves, Charles Burnett, and St. Clair Bourne directed their films outside the system. And an array of interesting dramatic stars came to the fore: Cicely Tyson and Paul Winfield in *Sounder* (1972); the queen and king of black romantic pop, Diana Ross and Billy Dee Williams, in *Lady Sings the Blues* (1972) and *Mahogany* (1975); Rosalind Cash in *Melinda* (1972); Diana Sands and Louis Gossett, Jr., in the underrated *The Landlord* (1970); Richard Pryor in *Which Way Is Up?* (1977), *Greased Lightning* (1977), and *Silver Streak* (1976).

The 1970s was an active, productive era, yet mainstream cinema still failed to offer the African-American audience a wide enough range of images, a diversity of cultural experiences. Too many action films were produced, not enough serious or offbeat dramas. By the time the era ended, the industry felt that the black film was dead; that indeed, in order for a black star to succeed, he or she had to appear in a "crossover" film that appealed to white audiences. And so the very black audience that race movies decades earlier had tried to reach was once again ignored.

By the 1980s, performers like Richard Pryor and Eddie Murphy became authentic box-office superstars, although in their Reagan-era crossover films their characters often func-

tioned in white worlds rather than in an African-American cultural context. By the close of the 1980s and start of the 1990s, such new independent filmmakers as Spike Lee and Robert Townsend surprised the industry when their low-budget features *She's Gotta Have It* (1986) and *Hollywood Shuffle* (1987) won favor with audiences and critics alike. If anything, these new films might well be viewed as a continuation of the race movie: here again were stories filmed specifically with a set of African-American cultural references and concerns that a black audience could immediately identify with and connect to. The films were also a blend of the type of entertainment and social concern that a filmmaker like Oscar Micheaux believed in: mass entertainment by black artists for the black audience. In the late 1980s, the independent black film went mainstream. There followed important films by such black filmmakers as Charles Burnett, John Singleton, Euzhan Palcy, Julie Dash, and Reginald Hudlin.

Today the old Hollywood films remain intact. But many of the race movies have vanished or been destroyed. Surviving films are often dated, mangled, and sweetly naïve, yet they remain vivid cultural artifacts, comments on black America's past, fantasies, obsessions, attitudes, and aspirations, a rare glimpse of the way black America was once willing to look at itself. Many of the later race films (as well as some of the more socially conscious earlier ones) succeeded best as fundamental celebrations of cultural roots and communal spirits—and also as pure, undiluted celebrations of black style. In such movies as *Broken Strings* (1940), *Boy! What a Girl* (1946), *Sepia Cinderella*, *The Bronze Buckaroo*, and scores of others, as well as in the work of African-American performers in certain Hollywood films, vocal inflections and intonations set the ears abuzz. The manners, gestures, postures, surprising double takes, swift interplay and communication between the characters is a world unto itself, capturing, despite whatever other distortions or failings, a segment of African-American life and culture.

The posters here, which were used in the past to promote or publicize the old films and which were often on display at theaters, capture some of the spirit and energy of that earlier black film history during the first half of the century. In some cases, they salute icons, touch on an era's mood and perspective, and bring us close to what a certain type of moviegoing experience was once like. Mainly, they open our eyes to a long line of past African-American filmmakers, entertainers, and artists leaping, struggling, or yearning, in the best and worst of situations, to make some kind of statement on film, their century's brave new medium.

—Donald Bogle

A SEPARATE CINEMA

WITHOUT A VOICE

P A R T O N E

The Norman Studios reunited Lawrence Criner and Kathryn Boyd after the mild success of *The Flying Ace* (1926). Along with Steve "Peg" Reynolds, a one-legged actor, they star in this true story about John Crisp and his struggle to secure oil in spite of the efforts of a crooked drilling contractor. The entire "all-colored city" of Tatums, Oklahoma, takes part in *Black Gold* and one scene, a fight between the hero and the villain, is staged on Main Street. Boyd did not survive the "talkies," but Criner continued as a featured player in the Lafayette Players Stock Company and in films, including *The Duke Is Tops* (1938), *Am I Guilty?* (1940), *Miracle in Harlem* (1948), and many others. He made his last film appearance in *The Jackie Robinson Story* (1950).

THE BULL-DOGGER
1923
Norman Film Manufacturing Company

Bill Pickett, an authentic black American cowboy and Wild West star of the Mexican bullring, is remembered as the "father of bull-dogging," the art of biting the tender part of a steer's lip and wrestling it to the ground, a technique he learned from watching his dog Spike herding cattle. Nicknamed "the Dusky Demon," Pickett hired Will Rogers and Tom Mix as his rodeo assistants in 1908 during their early days at the famous Miller Brothers 101 Ranch in Oklahoma. In 1921, at the age of fifty-nine, Pickett made the first of his two movies, *The Crimson Skull*, for Norman Films, but he appeared in a skeleton costume rather than in the chaps that made him famous enough to be inducted into the Black Cowboy Hall of Fame in 1971. (See page 2.)

THE FLYING ACE
1926
Norman Film Manufacturing Company
Courtesy of the Larry Richards Collection

Lawrence Criner, one of the original Lafayette Players, plays Captain Billy Stokes and Kathryn Boyd, also a Lafayette Player, is Ruth Sawtelle, a female daredevil. In her most daring escapade, Boyd, playing the scene herself, appears to climb a slender rope ladder suspended from a plane a mile up in order to escape from its burning fuselage (the scene was actually shot on the ground). Though heartily acclaimed in private press screenings, this first silent film to offer segregated theaters a look at airplane flight failed to attract black audiences.

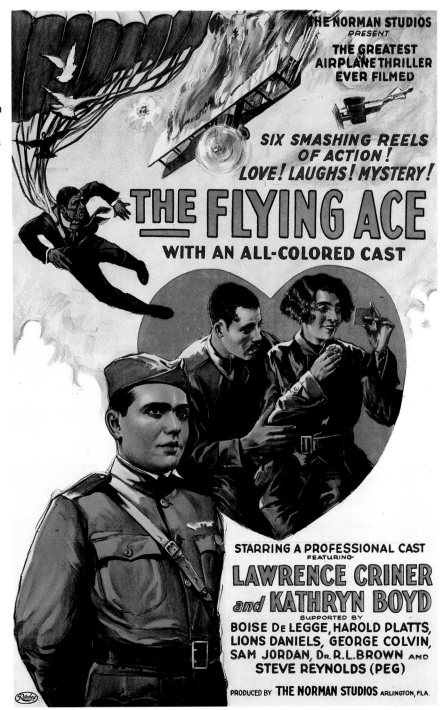

A CHOCOLATE COWBOY
1925
Cyclone Comedy
Courtesy of the Edward Mapp Collection

One of an early series of short films known as the Cyclone Comedies, the film attempted to fill the demand of African-American audiences for a black Western hero.

REGENERATION
1923
Norman Film Manufacturing Company

Given its inspirational title, filmgoers might have expected a profound story of spiritual rebirth, but the film is actually a black melodrama in the tradition of *Robinson Crusoe*. A woman and a man are cast upon an uninhabited island, a Garden of Eden. The plot includes romance, villainy, mystery, and action. The hero and heroine have light complexions; the villain is dark-skinned.

THE LURE OF A WOMAN
1921
Progress Picture Producing Association

In 1916 Noble Johnson founded the Lincoln Motion Picture Company with backing from the National Negro Business League in Kansas City, Missouri. After being funded, he went to California to set up his studio, leaving Missouri without an all-black-owned film production company. Four new film concerns were able to obtain financing in Kansas City in the early 1920s. Only two of them actually produced any films: the Andlauer Film Company's *As the World Rolls On* (1921), starring the well-known pugilist Jack Johnson, and the Progress Picture Producing Association's *The Lure of a Woman* (1921), co-starring Regina Cohee, Dr. A. Porter Davis, and Charles Allen in their only known film appearance. The two other companies, Gate City Feature Film Company and the Turpin Film Company, were inactive.

THE FLAMING CRISIS
1924
Monarch Productions

This black-owned production company from New York City is credited with having produced only one film. Calvin Nicholson plays a newspaperman who exposes a corrupt local labor leader with a lot of political power and is imprisoned unjustly for the labor leader's murder. After escaping from jail, he migrates to the cattle lands of the Southwest for a series of adventures before the film reaches an unexpected and amorous happy finale.

UNCLE TOM'S CABIN
1927
Universal
Courtesy of the
Bruce Hershenson Collection

UNCLE TOM'S CABIN
1958
Colorama

UNCLE TOM'S CABIN
1940s
Studio not known

UNCLE TOM'S CABIN
1940s
Studio not known

UNCLE TOM'S CABAÑA
1947
Metro-Goldwyn-Mayer
Courtesy of the Bruce Hershenson Collection

This parody of *Uncle Tom's Cabin* is deemed by many to be animator Tex Avery's finest cartoon. The liberties taken with the original story permit Uncle Tom to be run over with a steamroller and cut in half with a sawmill blade. Finally, in a moment of uncharacteristic militancy, he hurls Simon Legree into outer space tied to the Empire State Building.

UNCLE TOM'S CABIN
1969
Kroger Babb
Courtesy of the Edward Mapp Collection

Harriet Beecher Stowe's classic American novel about the good religious slave has been the source of numerous motion pictures commencing in 1902. The earlier versions cast a white actor in blackface as Tom. Finally, in 1914, the black actor Sam Lucas played Tom, followed in the 1927 version by another black actor, James B. Lowe. The 1927 film included a spectacular baptismal scene not seen in the previous versions. The film was reissued in 1958 with a prologue by the Canadian actor Raymond Massey.

PIONEERS OF INDEPENDENCE: OSCAR MICHEAUX AND SPENCER WILLIAMS

PART TWO

THE EXILE
1931
Micheaux Pictures Corporation

With *The Exile*, Oscar Micheaux became the first black director to produce a sound film. The story is an adaptation of his first novel, *The Conquest* (1913), about a black man who is in love with a woman he believes is white. Given his extremely limited shooting budget and the fact that recording dialogue was an expensive proposition, Micheaux packed the film with lengthy sequences of music and dance. Micheaux had not yet mastered the art of recording dialogue. Periodically the audience can hear his directions from behind the camera while the actors gesture him to be quiet. Micheaux's difficulty with recording dialogue is evident in several of his features.

THE GIRL FROM CHICAGO
1932
Micheaux Pictures Corporation

Oscar Micheaux produced an earlier version of this crime melodrama under the title *The Spider's Web* (1926). Carl Mahon plays a Secret Service agent in love with a schoolteacher played by Starr Calloway. A "numbers" man is murdered in New York, and Mahon's character becomes involved while aiding his friends. Juano Hernandez, who later gained recognition in Hollywood, makes his first film appearance. This poster supports the allegation that many of Micheaux's stars were selected on the basis of what in the vernacular of the day was referred to as their "high yellow" skin color.

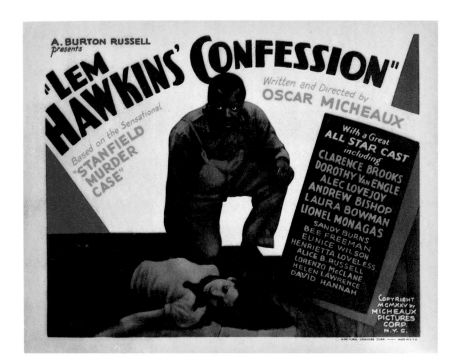

LEM HAWKINS' CONFESSION
1935
Micheaux Pictures Corporation

Based on Micheaux's novel *The Story of Dorothy Stanfield*, the film stars Clarence Brooks, the actor who played a Haitian doctor in Samuel Goldwyn's *Arrowsmith* (1932). In this black-cast film, he portrays a writer and law student, an uncommon status for a black character in films of the period. Brooks was a founder and feature player of the Lincoln Motion Picture Company, the first black-owned and -operated film corporation in the United States.

UNDERWORLD
1937
Micheaux Pictures Corporation
Courtesy of the Edward Mapp Collection

Micheaux offered a black perspective on the Chicago gangster film genre so popular in Hollywood. The film was not a box-office success, playing only four days in its initial release at the Harlem Opera House. Oscar Polk, one of its stars, gained a degree of recognition as Scarlett O'Hara's loyal servant in *Gone With the Wind* (1939).

MURDER IN HARLEM (LEM HAWKINS' CONFESSION)
1935
Micheaux Pictures Corporation

Under its original title, *Lem Hawkins' Confession*, this film opens with Lem Hawkins, a black night watchman, discovering the body of a young white woman. In classic flashback style, a story of spurned love, murder, and bribery unfolds. Clarence Brooks plays Henry Glory, an author selling his book door to door, paralleling experiences in Oscar Micheaux's own life. With the title *Murder in Harlem*, this film was lost to audiences until 1983, when prints of thirty important black-cast films were discovered in a warehouse in Tyler, Texas. Though Micheaux directed and wrote the screenplay, the film was produced by his wife, A. Burton Russell.

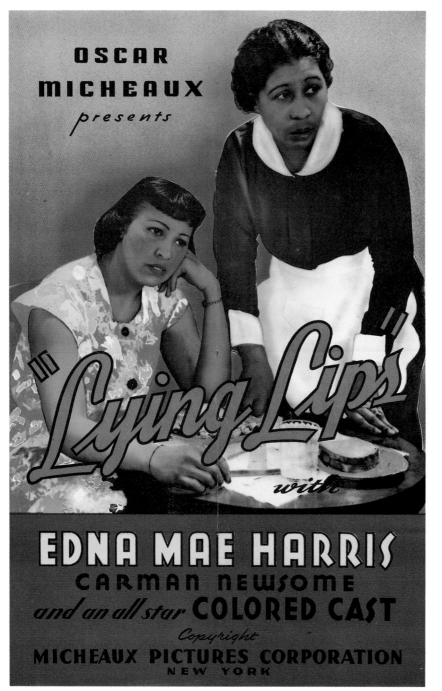

LYING LIPS
1939
Micheaux Pictures Corporation

One of Oscar Micheaux's better-known melodramas, *Lying Lips* was co-produced by the distinguished black aviator Colonel Hubert Julian. Edna Mae Harris plays a nightclub singer unjustly imprisoned and accused of murder. Juano Hernandez, who has a small part in the film, went on to act in Hollywood films such as *Intruder in the Dust* (1949) and *St. Louis Blues* (1958). Cast member Robert Earl Jones is the real-life father of actor James Earl Jones.

TEMPTATION
1936
Micheaux Pictures Corporation

In order to fully appreciate the ingenuity of Micheaux, one must remember that this film was made with a budget of only $15,000. This was only the second of the several Micheaux movies in which Ethel Moses starred. The film was an attempt to imitate the sophisticated Hollywood seduction melodramas made popular by Jean Harlow. In a typical Micheaux promotion campaign, Ethel Moses was touted as the "Negro Harlow" and her co-star, Lorenzo Tucker, as the "black Valentino."

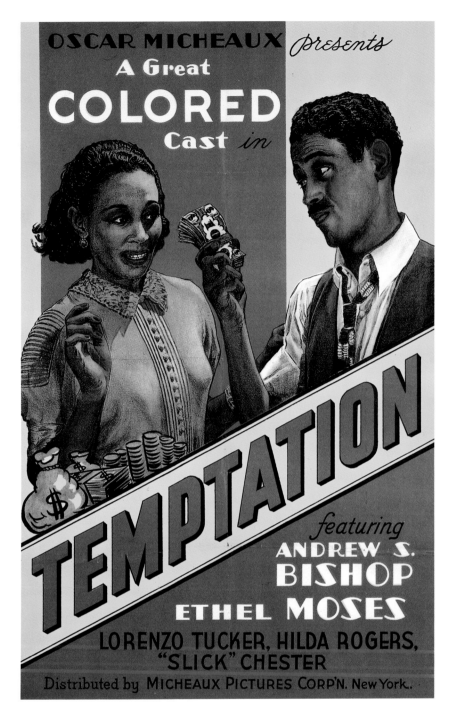

BIRTHRIGHT
1939
Micheaux Pictures Corporation

Inclined to adapt his screenplays from novels, Oscar Micheaux based this one on T. S. Stribling's novel of the same title about a black Harvard graduate confronting racism. The film's subtitle, *A Story of the Negro and the South*, referred to the young hero's efforts to found a school for black children in a small town in Tennessee in order to "uplift the race," a phrase Spike Lee used fifty years later as the subtitle for *School Daze*. Micheaux made an earlier, silent version of *Birthright* in 1924.

SWING
1938
Micheaux Pictures Corporation

Although Oscar Micheaux used a great deal of music in most of his dramatic films, it was usually to keep the audience tapping its feet until the social message could be delivered. *Swing*, on the other hand, was intended to be a musical. Micheaux does not always succeed in staying with his story line, but then again marital infidelity does seem like an unlikely topic for a musical. The Tyler Twins execute the dance numbers supported by a bevy of beautiful chorines.

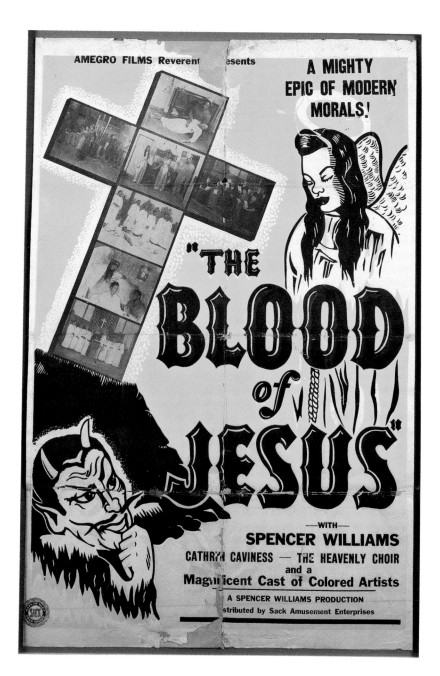

THE BLOOD OF JESUS
1941
Sack Amusement Enterprises
Courtesy of the Edward Mapp
Collection

Spencer Williams, who later became known as Andy on the *Amos 'n' Andy* television series, was the star, producer, director, and screenplay writer of this unusual story. The film provided a glimpse of Southern Baptist folk theology from an entirely black perspective. Due to the success of this film and Williams' great ability to control production, Alfred Sack offered him a ten-year association with his film company for eight more features.

SON OF INGAGI
1940
Sack Amusement Enterprises
Courtesy of the Larry Richards
Collection

The first black-cast horror film was scripted from an original short story, "House of Horror," by Spencer Williams, who also played a role in the movie. Dramatic stage actress Laura Bowman, an original member of the Lafayette Players Stock Company, had a leading part. Zack Williams, who was featured in *Gone With the Wind* the preceding year, played the ape-man. Ten years earlier a silent film made by Congo Pictures Limited introduced audiences to the original gorilla named Ingagi.

OF ONE BLOOD
1944
Sack Amusement Enterprises
Courtesy of the Glenn Bray Collection

Spencer Williams utilized the religious themes of *The Blood of Jesus* (1941) and *Go Down, Death* (1944) one final time, with poor results. As was his custom, Williams appeared in the film, playing a deaf-mute who turns out finally to be an undercover FBI agent.

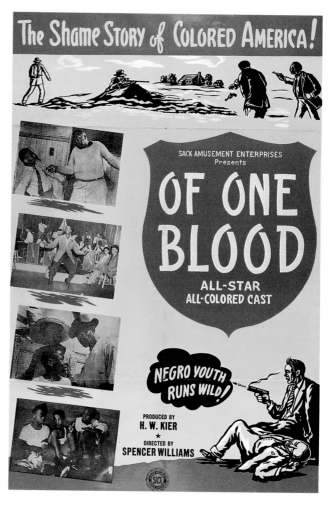

MARCHING ON!
1943
Sack Amusement Enterprises

One of the few black productions to deal with military life, this semi-documentary attempted to focus a much needed spotlight on the segregation of colored military personnel. But it became a piece of propaganda for the nation's war effort. In the 1950s additional footage of dancing girls was added to make the re-release, *Where's My Man To-Nite?*, a more marketable full-length feature.

GO DOWN, DEATH
1944
Sack Amusement Enterprises
Courtesy of the Larry Richards Collection

Written and directed by Spencer Williams, this fablelike drama subtitled *The Story of Jesus and the Devil* was inspired by a James Weldon Johnson poem of the same title. Following directly on the failure of his war drama *Marching On!* (1943), Williams hoped to duplicate the success of the earlier *The Blood of Jesus* (1941) by employing a similar Southern religious theme.

JUKE JOINT
1947
Sack Amusement Enterprises

This was Spencer Williams' last film. His work no longer dealt with folk religion and northward migration. Yet even in this stereotypical comedy, Williams includes a family-dinner prayer sequence out of respect for the black religious tradition. The film was shot in Texas on location in two different "joints," Don's Keyhole in San Antonio and the Rose Room in Dallas.

THE GIRL IN ROOM 20
1946
United Films
Courtesy of the Glenn Bray Collection

This not very well-known drama provides still another example of the duality of Spencer Williams as actor and director. Like Oscar Micheaux, Williams tended to use the same actors again and again. Robert Orr, a Texas dancer turned leading man, was known on the screen as July Jones in this as well as several other Spencer Williams features. The film was shot in San Antonio, Texas.

THE BETRAYAL
1948
Astor Pictures

Oscar Micheaux wrote a screenplay based on his novel *Wind from Nowhere* for this, the final film he produced and directed. The first all-black motion picture to have a Broadway premiere, it was shown twice daily on a reserved-seat basis. Even this strategy could not save the drama from critical as well as commercial failure. Micheaux, the most ingenious of early independent black filmmakers, died in 1951 in virtual oblivion.

HOLLYWOOD HIJINKS

PART THREE

HALLELUJAH
1929
Metro-Goldwyn-Mayer
Courtesy of the Steven Rebello Collection

Hollywood's second all-black-cast musical—*Hearts in Dixie* (1929) was the first—introduced sixteen-year-old Nina Mae McKinney singing Irving Berlin's "Swanee Shuffle." M-G-M did not make another film in this genre until *Cabin in the Sky* (1943). Victoria Spivey and the Dixie Jubilee Choir provide an exceptionally spiritual aura. Director King Vidor intended Paul Robeson to play the lead, but when he was unavailable, the role of Zeke was given to Daniel Haynes, then an understudy in *Show Boat*. The poster is by the artist Al Hirschfeld.

HEARTS IN DIXIE
1929
Fox
Courtesy of the Edward Mapp Collection

Although Clarence Muse was the star, movie audiences took note of Stepin Fetchit in this early film, which catapulted him to fame and riches as the consummate black comedic stereotype. His extraordinary timing and body language were well suited to the requirements of film. *Hearts in Dixie* has the distinction of being the first all-black-cast all-singing, all-talking musical to reach the screen.

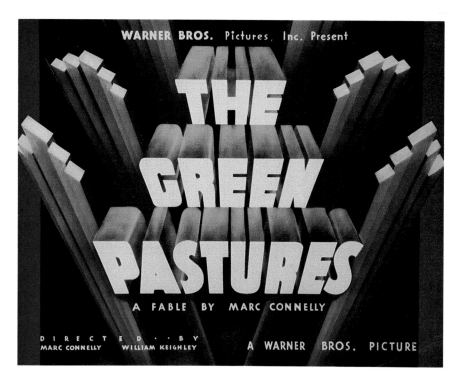

THE GREEN PASTURES
1936
Warner Brothers

Heavenly choirs, angel wings, and fish fries became metaphors for Hollywood's version of black folk life. This all-black-cast musical stars Rex Ingram in three roles, as De Lawd, Hezdrel, and Adam. It is hard to believe, but Al Jolson had wanted the part. Because this movie was made in the 1930s many people did not challenge the stereotyped image it presented. An array of talented actors breathed life into the characters, and many nonprofessionals were imported off the streets of Los Angeles and coached in the proper bayou accent.

THE GREEN PASTURES (Belgian version)
1936
Warner Brothers
Courtesy of the Edward Mapp Collection

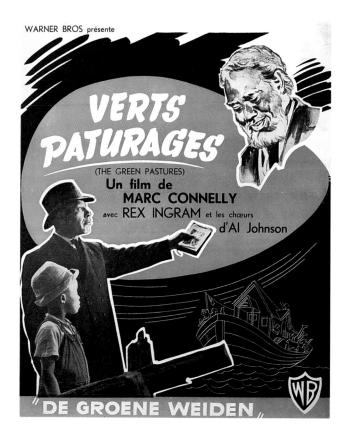

CABIN IN THE SKY
1943
Metro-Goldwyn-Mayer

Providing a much needed escape for movie audiences during World War II, this Vincente Minnelli film, his first for M-G-M, was an enjoyable musical fantasy about the eternal struggle of man caught between heaven and hell. Beginning her long-term contract with the studio, Lena Horne made an auspicious film debut as the seductress Georgia Brown. This film was so crowded with songs that one Louis Armstrong tune, "Ain't It the Truth," had to be edited in the film's final release. Considered a risky venture because of its all-black cast, the film was modestly budgeted for $680,000, the cheapest M-G-M musical production at the time. Eminent caricaturist Al Hirschfeld designed the posters.

CABIN IN THE SKY
1943
Metro-Goldwyn-Mayer

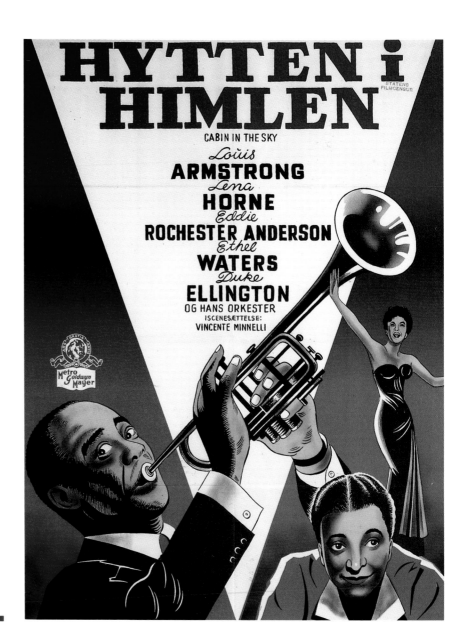

CABIN IN THE SKY
(Danish version)
1943
Metro-Goldwyn-Mayer

STORMY WEATHER
1943
20th Century–Fox
Courtesy of the Edward Mapp Collection

The title song provided a professional signature for Lena Horne's career and the film gave Bill "Bojangles" Robinson an opportunity to display his extraordinary terpsichorean skills without Shirley Temple. *Stormy Weather* is a love story with all of the expected complications. The director, Andrew Stone, who would later direct Dorothy Dandridge in *The Decks Ran Red* (1958), chose to release the film in sepia tone, adding an extra dimension to the exquisite photography. The production, with musical director Benny Carter, was all-star in every sense. Fats Waller, Cab Calloway, Ada Brown, Dooley Wilson, and the Nicholas Brothers were among the black entertainment luminaries. Horne's beauty became the central focus of all posters for this film.

STORMY WEATHER
1943
20th Century–Fox

CARMEN JONES
1954
20th Century–Fox

Dorothy Dandridge became the first black actress to receive an Acadamy Award nomination in the leading-role category, for her performance as Carmen Jones. The first all-black-cast musical since this studio's *Stormy Weather* (1943), Oscar Hammerstein's thrilling adaptation of Bizet's classic opera *Carmen* was a magnificent commercial success. The voices of Dandridge, Harry Belafonte, Joe Adams, and Diahann Carroll were dubbed for songs that included "Dat's Love," "Dis Flower," and "Dere's a Cafe on de Corner." Pearl Bailey performs "Beat Out That Rhythm on a Drum."

ST. LOUIS BLUES
1958
Paramount Pictures

With a lineup of popular and talented musicians and singers, this fictionalized biography of "the father of the blues," W. C. Handy, was patronizing and wasteful. The ever cool Nat "King" Cole, in the title role, gave an uncharismatic wooden performance that left the audience with only a slight taste of jazz. A very young Billy Preston portrays Handy as a child.

BLACK ORPHEUS
1959
Lopert Films (Brazil)

Based on the Greek Orpheus and Eurydice myth, this Marcel Camus film won the 1959 Cannes Film Festival Grand Prix. Both the original (Portuguese) and the dubbed (English) version attracted a wide audience. The carnival in Rio de Janeiro provides a beautiful backdrop for the story, as does the frenzied Brazilian musical theme, which became very popular.

PORGY AND BESS
1959
Columbia Pictures

An adaptation of George Gershwin's stage opera, this film won an Oscar for Andre Previn, its musical director. The singing voices of Sidney Poitier and Dorothy Dandridge were dubbed by Robert McFerrin and Adele Addison. Harry Belafonte allegedly rejected the opportunity to play Porgy, a role he would have had to perform on his knees. Poitier was effectively coerced by Samuel Goldwyn into taking the part in order not to lose the coveted role in *The Defiant Ones* (1958). The staunchly independent director Rouben Mamoulian, whose films include *Dr. Jekyll and Mr. Hyde*, *Queen Christina*, and *Silk Stockings*, was, for the second time in his career, replaced by Otto Preminger to helm a film.

PORGY AND BESS
(Belgian version)
1959
Columbia Pictures

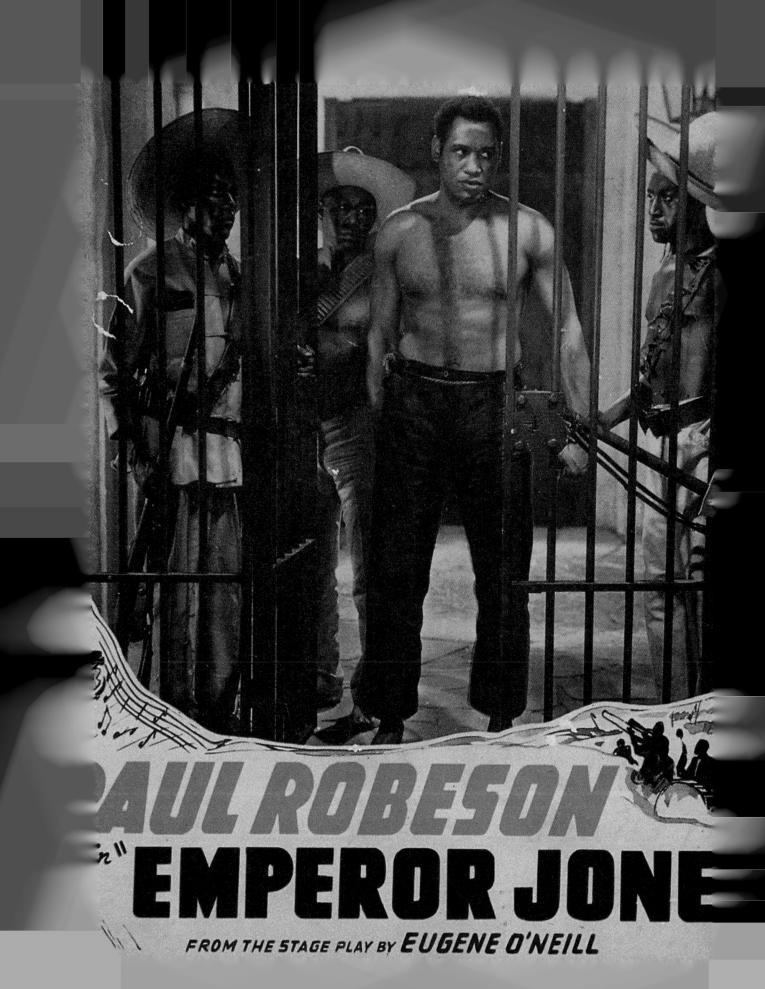

PAUL ROBESON

in "**EMPEROR JONE**

FROM THE STAGE PLAY BY **EUGENE O'NEILL**

A FILM ANACHRONISM: PAUL ROBESON

PART FOUR

THE EMPEROR JONES
1933
United Artists

Shot in one week on a shoestring budget of $10,000 at the Astoria Studios in Queens, New York, Paul Robeson's first commercial film, based on a play by Eugene O'Neill, has become a classic. He had already played the role on the Broadway and London stage. Those with sharp vision will notice appearances by Jackie "Moms" Mabley and Billie Holiday. J. Rosamond Johnson, who wrote "Lift Every Voice and Sing," was the film's musical director.

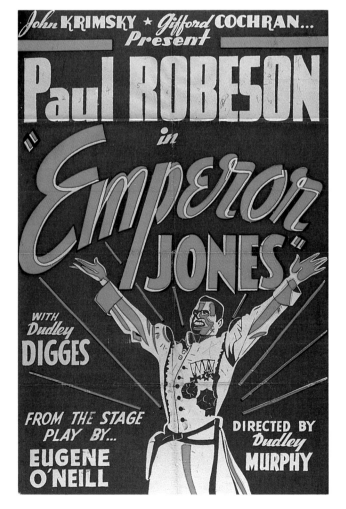

THE EMPEROR JONES
Reissue 1940
United Artists
Courtesy of the Glenn Bray Collection

THE SONG OF FREEDOM
1937
Lion-Hammer (England)
Courtesy of the Edward Mapp
Collection

Playing a dockworker turned opera singer and a long-lost royal heir to a small kingdom in Africa gave Robeson ample opportunity to display his rich singing voice and his acting skills, which had improved since his performance in the title role of *The Emperor Jones* (1933). Appearing as his wife is Elisabeth Welch, like Robeson a black American expatriate. It pleased Robeson to be able to imbue his characterization with some true aspects of the life of a black man.

BOSAMBO (SANDERS OF THE RIVER)
(Belgian version)
1935
Alexander Korda London Films
Courtesy of the Edward Mapp Collection

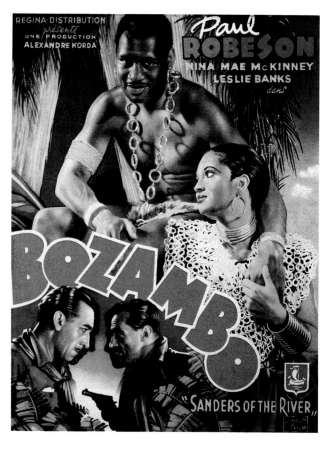

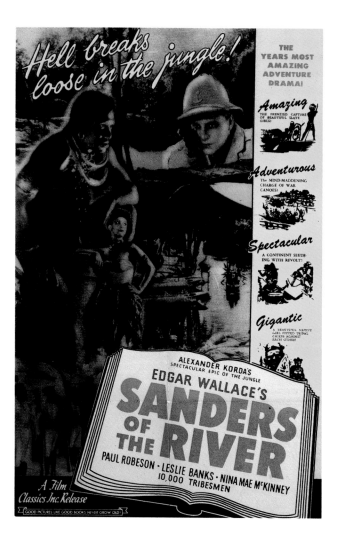

SANDERS OF THE RIVER
1935
Alexander Korda London Films

Unlike the Argentinian and Belgian versions, the American poster for the film downplays Robeson's presence. Since the plot primarily revolved around the character played by Robeson, *Bosambo* is a far more fitting title than *Sanders of the River*. Hoping to portray the role of an African leader with some cultural integrity and accuracy, the actor was disillusioned with the final edited movie, which presented Bosambo as merely a loyal servant of British colonialism. It is rumored that Robeson attempted to buy every print of the film to prevent its distribution.

BOSAMBO
(SANDERS OF THE RIVER)
(Argentinian version)
1935
Alexander Korda London Films
Courtesy of the Edward Mapp
Collection

KING SOLOMON'S MINES
(Argentinian version)
1937
Gaumont British Picture Company

Filmmakers recognized Paul Robeson's regality, if not consciously, then certainly subliminally. This was the second film in a year to cast him as a long-lost African king; *The Song of Freedom* was the other. Although the film was made on a London soundstage, supplementary scenic footage shot in Africa was incorporated. Robeson found the role of Umbopa in H. Rider Haggard's screenplay even less satisfying to play than that of Bosambo in Edgar Wallace's *Sanders of the River* (1935), although he was gratified to study Efik for cultural and linguistic authenticity.

DARK SANDS (JERICHO)
1937
Record Pictures Corporation

Filmed on location in Egypt, this film projected a forceful, heroic, and positive image of blacks. The main character is a wrongly accused black soldier who pursues personal justice. Robeson was proud that he was able to alter the script's original ending, which called for Jericho's emasculation. The leading lady, Princess Kouka, was discovered on location in an African village.

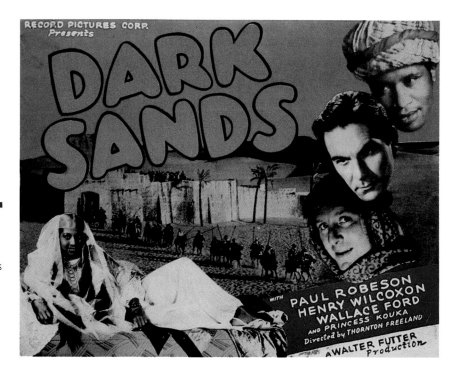

BIG FELLA
Lion-Hammer (England)

Loosely based on *Banjo* by Claude McKay, a noted Jamaican writer of the Harlem Renaissance period, the film is about a boy lost on the docks of Marseilles who is returned to his English parents. Robeson, in easygoing form for his modest title role, sings "Lazin'," "Roll Up, Sailorman," and "You Didn't Orta Do Such Things." Robeson's wife, Eslanda, plays a supporting role in the film, as does his longtime accompanist, Lawrence Brown.

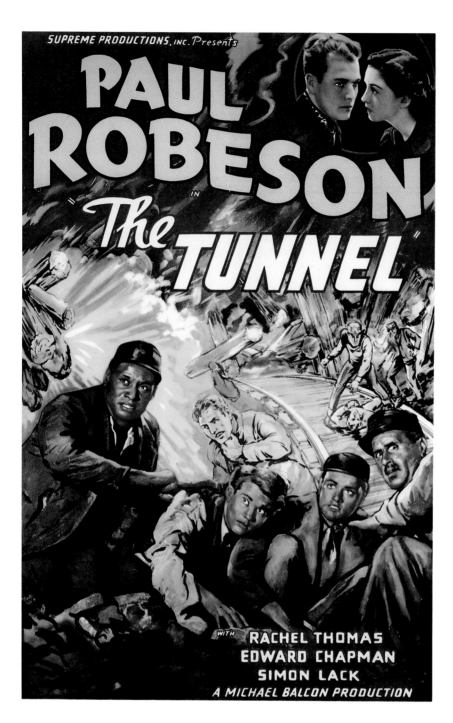

THE TUNNEL (THE PROUD VALLEY)
1940
Ealing (England)

**THE PROUD VALLEY
(THE TUNNEL)
(Danish version)
1940
Ealing (England)
Courtesy of the Edward Mapp
Collection**

The major asset of *Proud Valley* is the powerful Robeson voice rendering "Deep River," among other songs. The film is said to be Robeson's own personal favorite. Those who demur wonder why the sole black character, the stoker David Goliath, played by Robeson, must sacrifice his life for the unemployed Welsh miners whose coal pit he helps reopen.

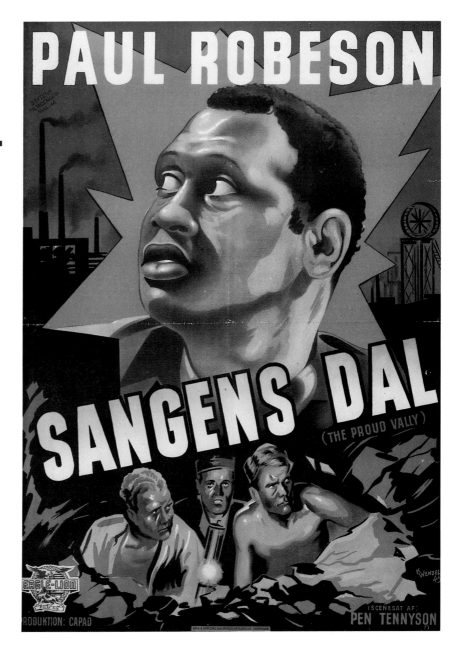

HARLEM GOES WEST

PART FIVE

TWO-GUN MAN FROM HARLEM
1938
Merit Pictures

The charlatan clergyman was a familiar character in black-cast movies of the 1930s, beginning with Paul Robeson's role as the rogue reverend in Oscar Micheaux's *Body and Soul* (1924). The phony deacon in this musical Western is transformed into a "shoot 'em up" cowboy. Ironically, Faithful Mary, a real-life disciple of Father Divine, the founder and leader of a peace-cult religious movement popular in the black community during the 1930s and 1940s, appears in the film. The Four Tones join Herb Jeffrey in providing musical interludes.

HARLEM RIDES THE RANGE
1939
Hollywood Productions

Spencer Williams wrote the script and played the villain in this all-black-cast Western musical about a family's control of a radium mine. In segregated theaters throughout the country, black children knew that Gene Autry might have his Champion, but their real hero, Herb Jeffrey, had his Stardusk. Ironically, Jeffrey's horse is white.

HARLEM ON THE PRAIRIE
1938
Associated Pictures

This film was made at N. B. Murphy's black dude ranch near Victorville, California. The three styles of posters were geared to entice different audiences by promoting the individual stars. When Ted Toddy re-released the film in the early 1940s, he spotlighted each star individually to capitalize on their popularity. Spencer Williams plays a gold thief who is shot by villains while trying to find his hidden cache. He seeks the aid of Herb Jeffrey (also spelled Jeffries), a young and trustworthy cowboy, to carry out the search along with Jeffrey's range-riding sidekick, Mantan Moreland.

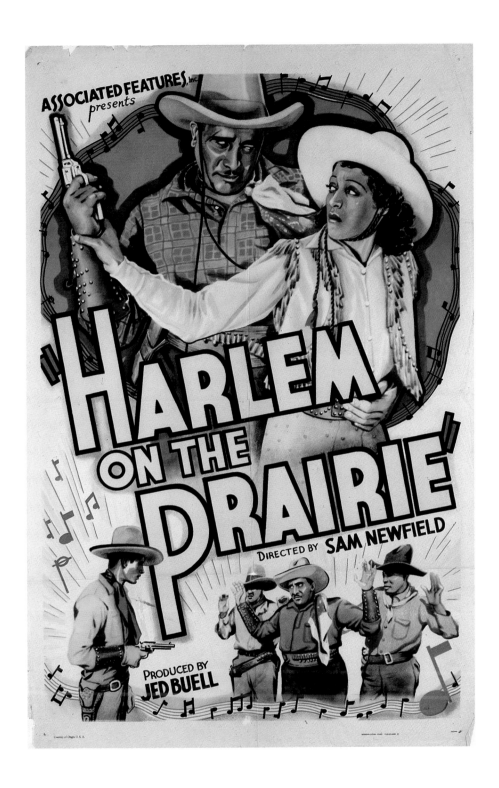

RHYTHM RODEO
1938
George Randol Productions
Courtesy of the Glenn Bray Collection

This musical Western, filmed on a ranch near Los Angeles, was the first for writer/ producer/director George Randol. Having finished *Harlem on the Prairie* the same year, Randol was now familiar with the Western motif and ready to create his own production company. Randol had previously served as co-director Marc Connelly's assistant on *The Green Pastures* (1936), and then as writer/co-director of musical shorts with the Hall Johnson Choir. In 1937 Randol produced and co-directed with Ralph Cooper the immensely popular *Dark Manhattan*. Due to fund-raising problems, he quit filmmaking after he produced and directed his third and final film, *Midnight Shadow*, in 1939.

THE BRONZE BUCKAROO
1938
Hollywood Productions
Courtesy of the Edward Mapp Collection

Bob Blake, the good cowpoke, played by Herb Jeffrey, and his sidekick, Dusty, played by Flournoy Miller, were characters much beloved by black children who spent Saturday afternoons in segregated (de facto in New York, de jure in Georgia) movie houses during the late 1930s. "Stout of heart, quick of eye, sweet of voice," the Bronze Buckaroo served as a role model for them. Earl Morris, a drama editor for *The Pittsburgh Courier*, a major black newspaper, played a small part in the film.

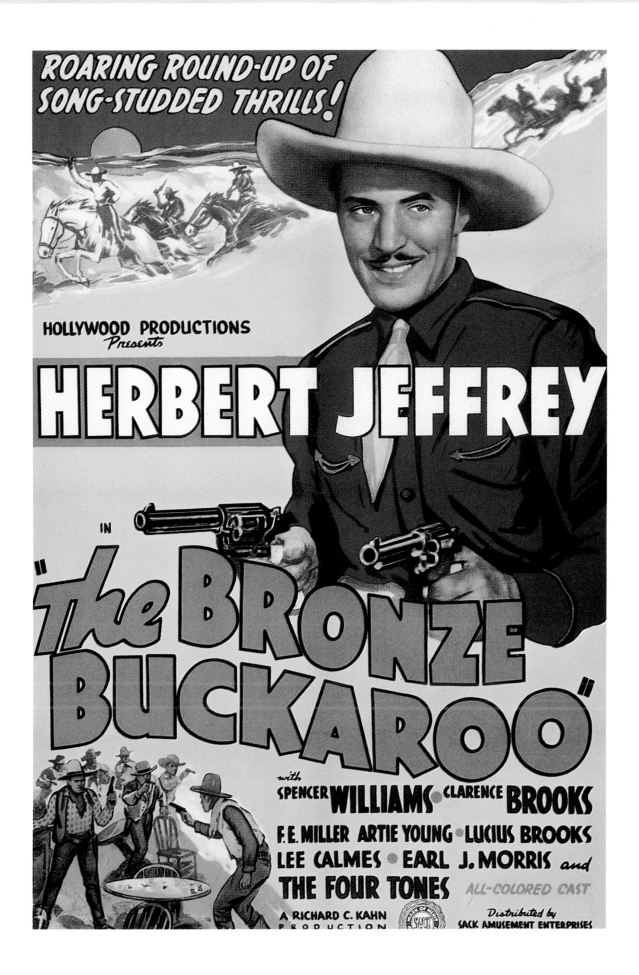

COME ON, COWBOY!
1948
Toddy Pictures

Comic Mantan Moreland teamed up in this raunchy Western with Johnny Lee, who later became known as attorney Algonquin J. Calhoun on the *Amos 'n' Andy* television series. Moreland and Lee were both experts at a comedy routine in which two people converse without completing their sentences yet enjoy a harmonious mutual understanding. Moreland appeared in over 300 movies and is best remembered for his work in Hollywood, particularly his role as Birmingham Brown, the chauffeur sidekick in the Charlie Chan mystery series.

LOOK-OUT SISTER
1946
Astor Pictures

Louis Jordan, who had acquired a large following of fans, both black and white, by virtue of his recordings with his group, the Tympany Five, turned to directing and starring in this Western. Paul Quinichette and Bill Doggett help Jordan perform "My New Ten-Gallon Hat," "Jack, You're Dead," and "Don't Burn the Candle at Both Ends," among other songs.

ROAR
OF THE
CROWD

WITH THE ONE AND ONLY
JOE LOUIS

HIS RISE — HIS FALL — HIS COMEBACK

Sensational Movietone Biography of The
Million Dollar Fighter With The
Great Ring Celebrities—
BAER - CARNERA - LEVINSKY
SCHMELING - SHARKEY - ETTORE
BRADDOCK

THRILL WITH THE MILLIONS!
ROAR WITH THE CROWD

A Double Barreled Program Shown With
Extra Feature And Comedy

=== YOU'LL LIKE IT ===

A GIFT OF THE GODS

PART SIX

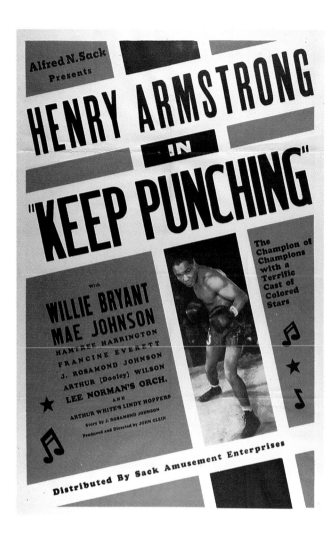

KEEP PUNCHING
1939
Sack Amusement Enterprises
Courtesy of the Glenn Bray Collection

Henry Armstrong, the only pugilist ever to hold three championship titles (lightweight, featherweight, and welterweight), was a natural box-office attraction in this black-cast sports melodrama. Armstrong's acting limitations were counterbalanced by the casting of a roster of talented African-American thespians, including Alvin Childress, Canada Lee, Dooley Wilson, and Francine Everett, making her film debut as the heroine.

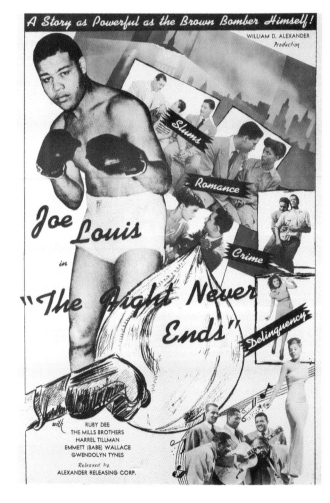

THE FIGHT NEVER ENDS
1947
Alexander Productions
Courtesy of the Edward Mapp Collection

Nine years earlier, heavyweight boxing champion of the world Joe Louis made his acting debut in *The Spirit of Youth*. In this, his second film, Louis plays himself. A brief appearance by the Mills Brothers added some musical flavor. The black-and-red duotone poster was made for the Toddy Pictures re-release in 1948.

THE JOE LOUIS STORY
1953
United Artists

Actual footage of some of Joe Louis' bouts, including those against Max Baer, Max Schmeling, and Billy Conn, was interspersed in this fictionalized account covering two decades of his life. Although Louis appeared in two other black-cast films during the 1930s and 1940s, *The Spirit of Youth* (1938) and *The Fight Never Ends* (1947), he was now too old to star. Coley Wallace, an ex–Golden Gloves fighter and a nonprofessional actor, plays the Brown Bomber. Hilda Simms, who performed the title role in *Anna Lucasta* (1944) on Broadway, plays Marva Louis, his estranged wife. Simms never hit her stride in films; as a mulatto she did not fit the Hollywood mold of black actress. James Edwards, the distinguished Broadway actor and lead in the Stanley Kramer hit *Home of the Brave* (1949), is fight trainer "Chappie" Blackburn. The Ellis Larkin Trio plays the theme song, "I'll Be Around."

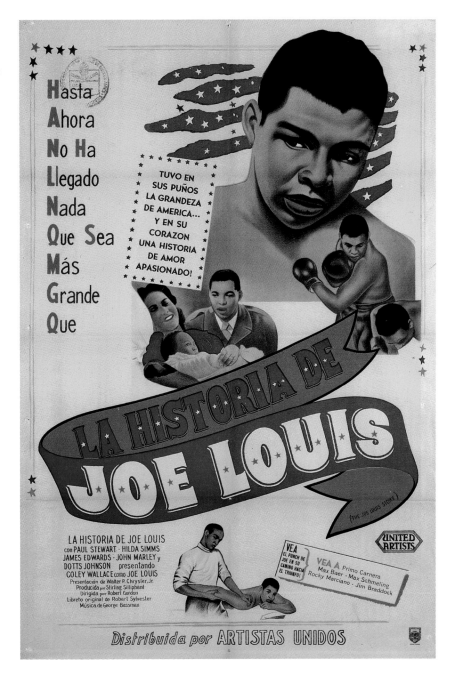

ROAR OF THE CROWD
1953
Monogram Pictures

This biographical documentary allowed Joe Louis fans and black movie audiences to view Louis without the contrived plots and mediocre acting of other films about the Brown Bomber. In segregated society, Louis was a role model for black kids. He turned pro in 1934 and from then until he came out of retirement in 1950 he suffered only one defeat; in 1936 Max Schmeling knocked him out in twelve rounds. Adolf Hitler used Schmeling's victory as propaganda for Aryan supremacy. In a rematch, Louis unleashed his pent-up fury and knocked out Schmeling in the first round. Louis still holds the record as the longest-reigning heavyweight: eleven years and eight months as champ. (See page 58.)

GO, MAN, GO!
1954
United Artists

This sports melodrama represented a special brand of film exploitation. Counting on the drawing power of black athletes, the Harlem Globetrotters in this case, a producer would assume that a low-budget, hastily prepared production would satisfy loyal fans. This was the only feature film to be directed by veteran photographer James Wong Howe. The title song, composed by Sy Oliver and sung by Slim Gaillard, and an early performance by Sidney Poitier are among the film's assets.

CROOKED MONEY
(WHILE THOUSANDS CHEER)
1940
Toddy Pictures

In a classic example of typecasting, Kenny Washington, former UCLA All-American football star, plays a clean-cut young college athlete trying to distance himself from unwanted criminal interference in varsity sports. Mantan Moreland has a minor role in this melodrama. The film was also distributed under the title *Gridiron Graft*.

**THE JACKIE ROBINSON
STORY**
1950
Eagle-Lion
**Courtesy of the Edward Mapp
Collection**

The first black player in major-league baseball was an appropriate subject for this low-budget Hollywood film of the post–World War II era. Robinson played himself. His success in breaking baseball's "color bar" in 1947 had earned him international celebrity status. Former All-American football player Kenny Washington had a small role in the film.

COMIC, COON, OR BUFFOON?

PART SEVEN

LAFF JAMBOREE
1945
Toddy Pictures

Ford Washington Lee and John William Sublett were a comedy and song-and-dance duo known as Buck and Bubbles. They started working together as young boys in Louisville, Kentucky, doing odd jobs for the circus, riding horses at Churchill Downs, and after the start of World War I, playing ball for the Louisville Colonels, a baseball team managed by future Yankee manager Joe McCarthy. At the end of the season they joined an all-black troupe touring the South, with Buck (Lee) at the piano and Bubbles (Sublett) dancing the "sand dance," a rhythmic shuffle over an area lightly sprinkled with sand in which the dancer's feet never leave the ground. In 1921, Nat Nazarro, a vaudeville star in New York, picked up their act as his encore. After a five-year contract expired, they went off on their own, touring the United States and Europe. Audiences that were not privileged to see them at the Ziegfeld Follies, at the Palace Theatre, or during their two-week sold-out performance at the London Palladium in 1931 could discover their essence in these films. The two films made in 1929 were directed by William Foster, a pioneer black filmmaker in Chicago.

HIGH TONES
1929
Pathé

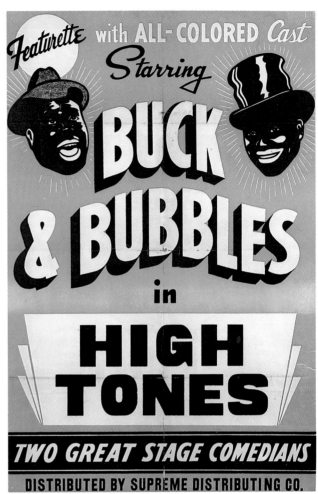

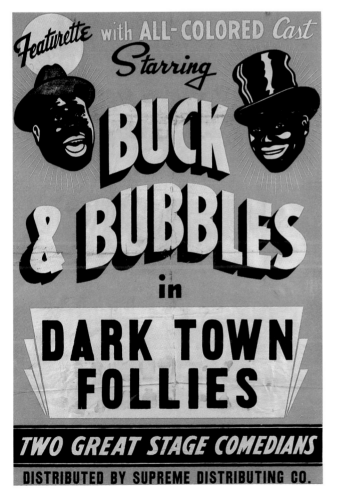

DARK TOWN FOLLIES
1929
Pathé

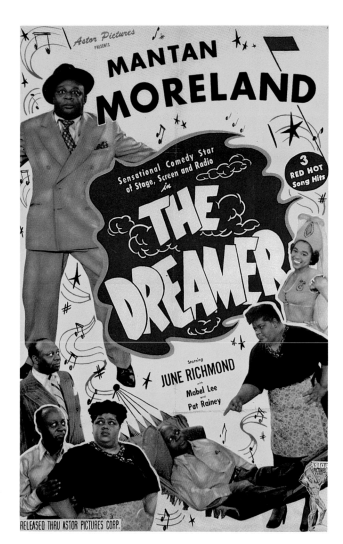

THE DREAMER
1948
Astor Pictures

In a feature role, Big Band vocalist June Richmond sings "All You Want to Do Is Eat" and "My Man Is Working Again." Before appearing in this film, Richmond had been, at various times, a featured singer with Les Hite, Jimmy Dorsey, Cab Calloway, and Andy Kirk's Clouds of Joy.

PROFESSOR CREEPS
1941
Dixie National Productions

Professionally, black comedian Mantan Moreland led a dual life. He achieved mainstream recognition and ridicule as Birmingham Brown, the chauffeur in the Charlie Chan series, while at the same time starring in all-black-cast productions, like this one, where he traded big salaries for better roles and top billing. Moreland's career began in circuses, road companies, and tent shows before Joe Louis got him an important role in *The Spirit of Youth* (1937).

LUCKY GHOST
1941
Dixie National Productions
Courtesy of the Glenn Bray Collection

The Ted Toddy organization in New York, along with Jed Buell and James Frederick from Dixie National Productions in Atlanta, produced numerous black-cast comedies in the early 1940s starring Mantan Moreland. Financed from Toddy's Westerns and other all-black-cast features, the films limited the talented Moreland to wide-eyed buffoonery, and on the whole were as demeaning as Hollywood films of the same variety. Black critics often gave these "race movies" negative reviews, but they were very popular with the segregated audiences for whom they were made. *Lucky Ghost* was a sequel to *Mr. Washington Goes to Town* (1940). Moreland's great ambition to do a "serious" piece of theater was finally realized in 1957 when he was cast as Estragon in an all-black New York production of *Waiting for Godot*.

SHE'S TOO MEAN FOR ME
1948
Toddy Pictures

In his bug-eyed stereotypical fashion, Mantan Moreland was the master of the double take. His black films set him up as something of a comic, sporty ladies' man. In this one, infidelity is the basis for a typically comic story. Moreland died in 1973 and was inducted posthumously into the Black Filmmakers' Hall of Fame in 1984.

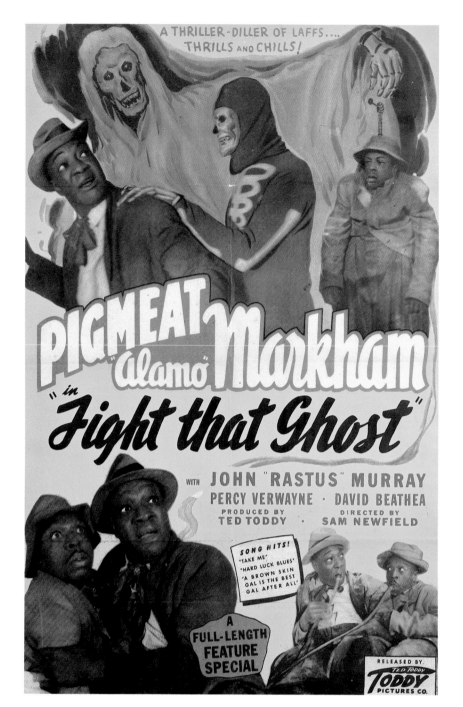

FIGHT THAT GHOST
1946
Toddy Pictures

The black comedian's exaggerated fear of ghostly apparitions was a popular cinematic shtick not only in Hollywood films but also in many white-produced black-cast films such as this one. Early in his career, Dewey Markham, the film's star, performed in a minstrel show in which Count Basie was the pianist. A song from those days, "Sweet Papa Pigmeat," gave Markham the nickname "Pigmeat," with which he was to become permanently identified.

HOUSE-RENT PARTY
1946
Toddy Pictures
Courtesy of the Larry Richards
Collection

The "rent party" tradition originated in the South with church socials designed to raise money. In Harlem the concept was refined. Someone's apartment with the lights down low, the soul food piled high, and one of uptown's top-stride pianists flailing at the keys of a dilapidated upright was the place to really let loose. A veteran of over a dozen all-black-cast comedies, Dewey "Pigmeat" Markham achieved his greatest recognition not in films but in front of black audiences at vaudeville venues. His trademark was "Here comes de judge," later popularized for white audiences on the television show *Laugh-In* in the late 1960s.

DRESS REHEARSAL
1939
Sepia-Art Pictures Co.

This was the first featurette to be produced by the Sepia-Art Pictures Co., which Eddie Green founded in New York City in 1939. It was also the first black-cast film to be shown on network television; NBC aired it in 1940. A magician and a Minsky burlesque comic for years, Green later became known as "Eddie the waiter" on radio's *Duffy's Tavern* series.

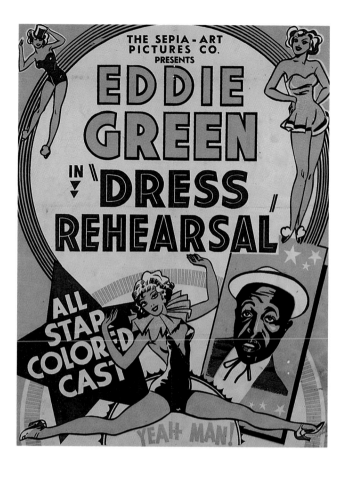

COMES MIDNIGHT
1940
Sepia-Art Pictures Co.

The second featurette produced by this black-owned company starred James Baskett, who later earned fame and an Oscar for his role as Uncle Remus in Walt Disney's *Song of the South* (1947). Appearing with him in *Comes Midnight* was Amanda Randolph, who became better known as the mother-in-law of Kingfish on the *Amos 'n' Andy* television series.

BIG TIMERS
1940
All-American News, Inc.
Courtesy of the Edward Mapp Collection

Lincoln Theodore Monroe Andrew Skeeter Perry gained fame as Stepin Fetchit, who personified the lazy, slow servant in numerous American films. Fetchit also brought his stereotypical antics to a small number of independent black productions such as this one, but the other black characters in *Big Timers* provided the realistic balance that was missing from his high-salaried mainstream films.

BOARDING HOUSE BLUES
1948
All-American News, Inc.

A farfetched plot allows the various entertainers in the cast, including Dusty Fletcher and Jackie "Moms" Mabley, to show off their talents. This vaudeville show on film is one of only five movies in which Mabley appeared during her lengthy career, dressed as always in old-time cotton print dresses and addressing her audience as "my chillens." She became successful during the Harlem Renaissance, appearing in clubs for $85 a week. By the 1960s the comic methods which insulated her audience from the harsh realities of the outside world brought her a salary of $8,500 a week. Dusty Fletcher was best known for his "Open the Door, Richard" routine, in which his only props were his ill-fitting clothes and a ladder that he would drunkenly attempt to climb, all the while hollering a comic monologue to a fictitious friend who has locked him out. Fletcher's stage popularity earned him roles in several films.

**GONE ARE THE DAYS!
(THE MAN FROM
C.O.T.T.O.N.)
1963
Trans Flux
Courtesy of the Edward Mapp
Collection**

Ossie Davis, as Reverend Purlie, co-stars with his wife, Ruby Dee, in his screenplay of his own Broadway hit, *Purlie Victorious*. Alan Alda, who later became famous for his role on the television program *M*A*S*H*, is one of two white actors to be featured in the film. The alternate title was an attempt to achieve wider distribution for this satire of Southern behavior in the era of *The Man from U.N.C.L.E.* television show.

BRONZE FEMMES FATALES

PART EIGHT

PRINCESS TAM-TAM
1935
Les Films H. Roussillon (France)
Courtesy of the Jay Levine Collection

Born in St. Louis, Missouri, in 1906 to a poor washerwoman, Josephine Baker grew up fatherless. She worked her way to New York to appear in the Broadway chorus line of Eubie Blake and Noble Sissle's musical comedy *Shuffle Along* (1922) followed by a Broadway production of *Chocolate Dandies* (1924) and a floor show at the Plantation Club featuring Ethel Waters. Offered $250 a week to star in *La Revue Nègre* (1924), Baker was soon on her way to Paris, where the wave of French enthusiasm for "Le Jazz Hot" brought her international fame as an expatriate. Baker left the show over a salary dispute and joined the Folies-Bergère, where she appeared as "Dark Star," a sensational role that had her dancing naked except for a G-string made of rubber bananas. In 1927 Baker was contracted to make her first film, *La Sirène des Tropiques*. The well-known French novelist Maurice Dekobra wrote the script that was designed to display Josephine Baker's special talents. She was cast as Papitou, a young West Indian girl who stows away on a steamship bound for Paris, where she sings and dances in the music halls for profit, naturally. The 1929 American premiere at the Lafayette Theater in Harlem featured the Joe Jordan Orchestra and a choir of twenty furnishing synchronized accompaniment for the film before a packed house that included New York City's mayor, Jimmy Walker. The film was considered by most critics to have been a waste of time for Baker.

With the success of a world tour behind her, Baker returned to Paris. She debuted at the Casino de Paris as a singing and dancing comedienne. Without abandoning her career, she also founded a nightclub, Chez Josephine, that quickly became the toast of Parisian society. Her next film, a talkie, *Zouzou* co-starred romantic French actor Jean Gabin, in his first role, and features Baker as a laundress who becomes a music-hall star. In 1935 Baker starred in *Princess Tam-Tam*, a light romance partially filmed in Tunisia. Baker plays an African beauty who is passed off on Parisian society as a princess. This Pygmalion fantasy was written by Pepito Abatino, who was Baker's longtime manager and confidant. One of the most beautiful songs from the film, "Le Chemin du Bonheur" (Dream Ship), was written by the famous early jazz composer Spencer Williams (no relation to the actor), who had previously worked with Baker on all of the music for *La Revue Nègre* in 1924. Films were a temporary diversion for Baker whose real niche was the music halls and cabarets. Her subsequent visits to the United States in the 1930s and 1940s fell far below her usual standards for success and were marred several times by racism. Baker became a naturalized French citizen in 1937. Her work in a fourth movie, *Fausse Alerte*, was cut short by the outbreak of World War II but was subsequently shown in the U.S.A. as *The French Way*.

LA SIRÈNE DES TROPIQUES
1927
Gold Talking Pictures (France)
Courtesy of the Windham/Silva Archives

(See page 76.)

ZOUZOU
1934
Marc Allegret Films (France)

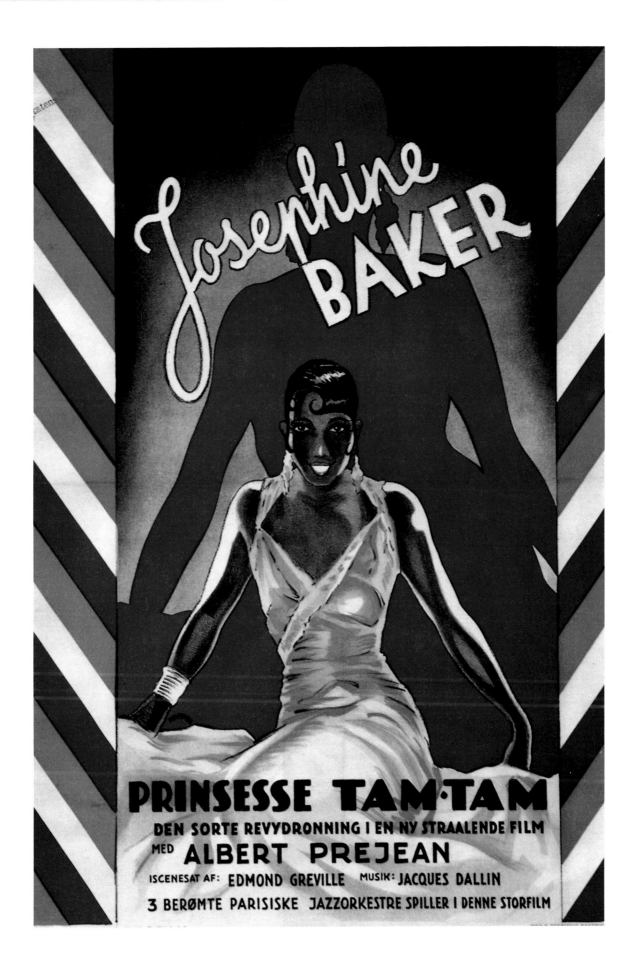

THE DUKE IS TOPS
1938
Million Dollar Pictures
Courtesy of the Glenn Bray Collection

THE BRONZE VENUS
(THE DUKE IS TOPS)
1943
Toddy Pictures

THE BRONZE VENUS
(THE DUKE IS TOPS)
1943
Toddy Pictures

Originally released as *The Duke Is Tops* (1938), the film was retitled to capitalize on Lena Horne's Hollywood success in two 1943 musicals, *Cabin in the Sky* and *Stormy Weather*. The posters present Horne and leading man Ralph Cooper as glamorous stars while simultaneously negating their blackness. Posters for the many M-G-M musicals Horne went on to perform in seemed dedicated to maintaining her invisibility. If the studio felt that Horne's presence might offend Southern audiences, her scenes were simply cut.

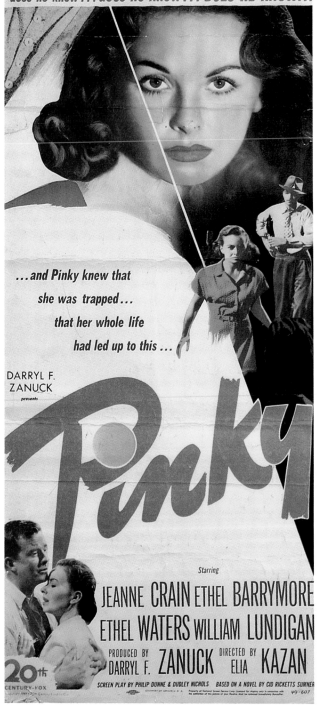

PINKY
1949
20th Century–Fox
Courtesy of the Edward Mapp Collection

The theme of "passing" had not been treated by a Hollywood film since *Imitation of Life* (1934). Although light-complexioned African-American actresses were available, Darryl Zanuck cast a white actress, Jeanne Crain, as Pinky. Her appearance detracted from the reality of the interracial situations since movie audiences knew they were not watching a black woman. John Ford, who was attempting to elicit an "Aunt Jemima" performance from Ethel Waters in the role of Dicey, was replaced by Elia Kazan as director. Attempts to censor the film in Texas were struck down in a 1952 Supreme Court decision.

PINKY
1949
20th Century–Fox
Courtesy of the Dawn Wheeler Collection

BUBBLING OVER
1934
RKO Radio Pictures
Courtesy of the Glenn Bray
Collection

Nicknamed "Sweet Mama Stringbean" because of her slender figure, Ethel Waters in the 1930s was a dramatic star of the stage as well as a most highly regarded singer, influencing Lena Horne and many others. *Rufus Jones for President* (1933), starring eight-year-old Sammy Davis, Jr., and *Bubbling Over* are the only two all-black-cast comedy shorts she made during her long career. A highlight of this film about life in a Harlem tenement is Waters singing "Darkies Never Cry," "Harlem Express," and "Taking Your Time." Waters was still projecting an unmistakable sexuality, which in her later mainstream films like *Pinky* (1949) and *The Member of the Wedding* (1952) was converted into an "earth mother" quality.

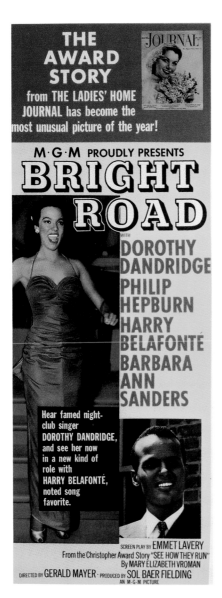

BRIGHT ROAD
1953
Metro-Goldwyn-Mayer

This low-budget, almost all-black, and often forgotten film is based on the Mary Elizabeth Vroman story "See How They Run," which *The Ladies' Home Journal* published in 1951 to nationwide acclaim. Dorothy Dandridge, who was already a famous singer and dramatic actress, plays a fourth-grade teacher whose understanding enables a rebellious pupil to find himself, and Harry Belafonte plays a school principal. In black communities the poster's advertising was often altered to refer to reviews by *Ebony* rather than reviews from more mainstream magazines. Dandridge and Belafonte would co-star only a year later in the widely acclaimed musical *Carmen Jones*.

TAMANGO
1959
A Hal Roach Release

A casual glance at the poster gives the false impression that *Tamango* was an exploitation film; it was actually a beautifully photographed first-class production, based on a work by the nineteenth-century French author Prosper Mérimée (also the source for *Carmen Jones*). One of Dorothy Dandridge's three final films, *Tamango* presented her as little more than an exotic sex object. Her tormented private life gave her film persona a haunting quality that is not easily forgotten.

ISLAND IN THE SUN
(Spanish version)
1957
20th Century–Fox

Miscegenation, murder, and interracial romance were the focus of this controversial film beautifully photographed in Barbados. Regretfully, the poster promises more than the film is willing to deliver on a sensitive subject. Dandridge, who is given little to do, looks incredibly beautiful.

NEW FACES
1954
20th Century–Fox

NEW FACES
(Danish version)
1954
20th Century–Fox

Eartha Kitt, the dusky chanteuse and former Katherine Dunham dancer, made her screen debut in the film version of this very popular 1952 stage revue. The only black in the cast, Kitt was anything but a "new face," thanks to hit records and the legacy of an Orson Welles remark. As her director in a jazzed-up production of *Faust* on the Paris stage, Welles proclaimed her "the most beautiful woman in the world."

ANNA LUCASTA
1958
United Artists

Eartha Kitt, whose film persona was primarily that of the femme fatale chanteuse, assumed the title role in one of the rare all-black dramas to be filmed during this period. In addition to co-star Sammy Davis, Jr., it features a roster of extremely talented black actors, including Rex Ingram, Frederick O'Neal, Rosetta Lenoire, and Alvin Childress. The 1949 film version, starring Paulette Goddard, was about a Polish family.

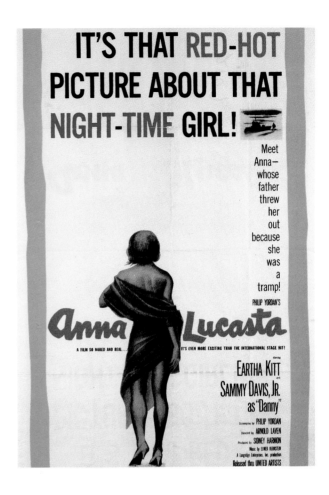

ANNA LUCASTA
(Belgian version)
1958
United Artists

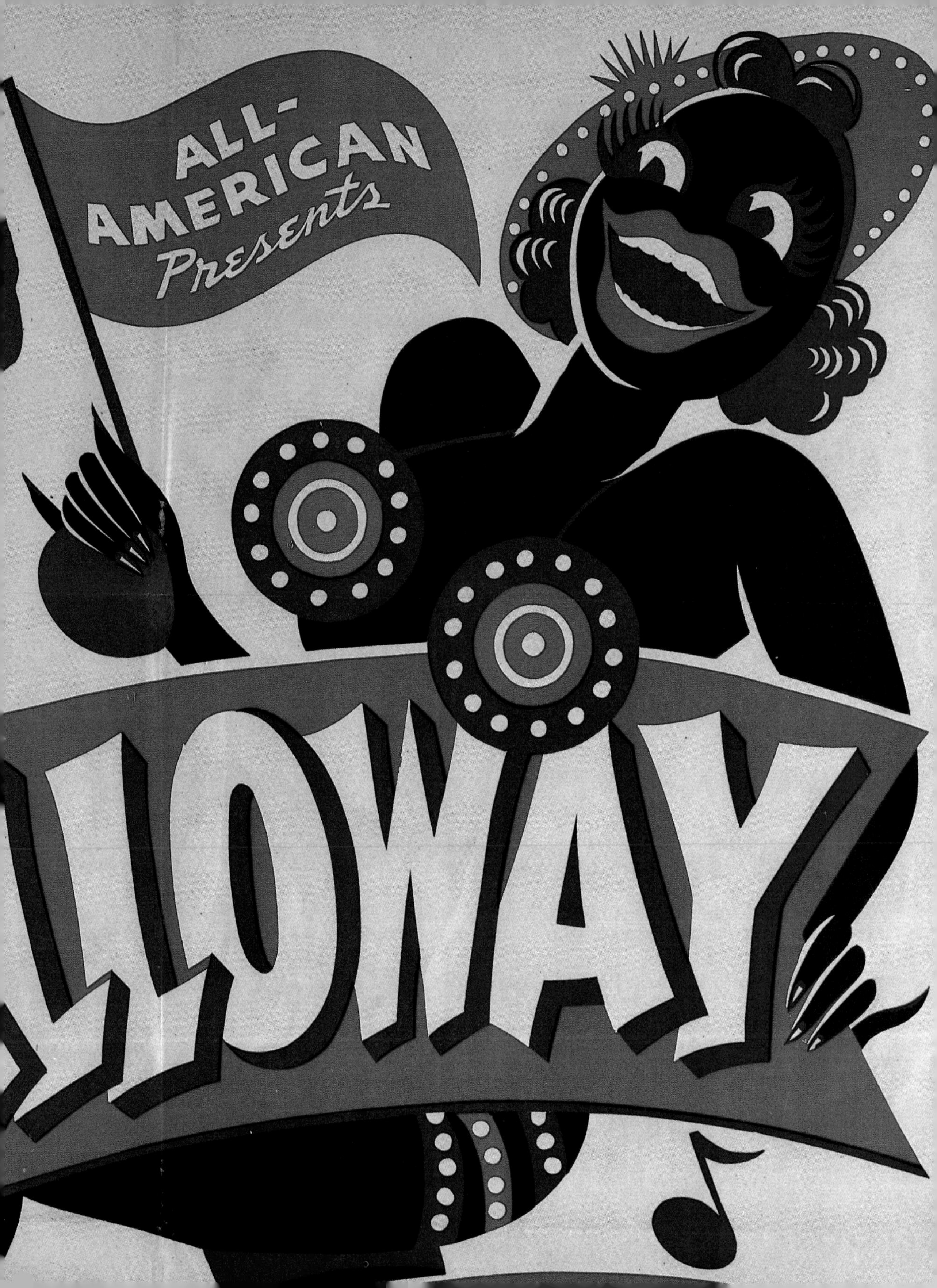
ALL-
AMERICAN
Presents
LLOWAY

JAZZIN', JAMMIN', AND JIVIN'

PART NINE

BLACK AND TAN
1929
RKO Radio Pictures
Courtesy of the Mitchell Diamond Collection

In 1927, when King Oliver and his band left the Cotton Club because of financial differences, Duke Ellington replaced him as the house band. He soon made it the most famous club in the world. Following that success, this musical short provided Duke Ellington with his first film appearance. *Black and Tan* was primarily a showcase for Ellington's piano playing. His leading lady, Fredi Washington, was soon to receive recognition as a dramatic actress in Fanny Hurst's *Imitation of Life* (1934). Director Dudley Murphy had previously made *St. Louis Blues* (1929) with Bessie Smith and would go on to make *The Emperor Jones* (1933). Among the numbers played by Ellington and his famous Cotton Club Orchestra were "The Duke Steps Out," "Black Beauty," "Hot Feet," and of course "Black and Tan Fantasy."

ST. LOUIS BLUES
1929
Sack Amusement Enterprises
Courtesy of the Mitchell
Diamond Collection

Bessie Smith, who never played in a "white" club, was earning $800 a week, in addition to $1,000 a recording in the 1920s. This seventeen-minute short film shot in Astoria, Queens, in New York City, is "the Empress of the Blues'" only screen role. She plays a wronged wife. Co-produced by W. C. Handy, author of the title song, the film also featured Isabel Washington (sister of Fredi Washington), who plays the "other woman." The music was provided by James P. Johnson and the Hall Johnson Choir. The overwhelming pathos of Smith's singing makes this a true film classic. During the Depression, Columbia Records was forced to cancel her contract, effectively ending her career. A car accident claimed her life in Mississippi in 1937.

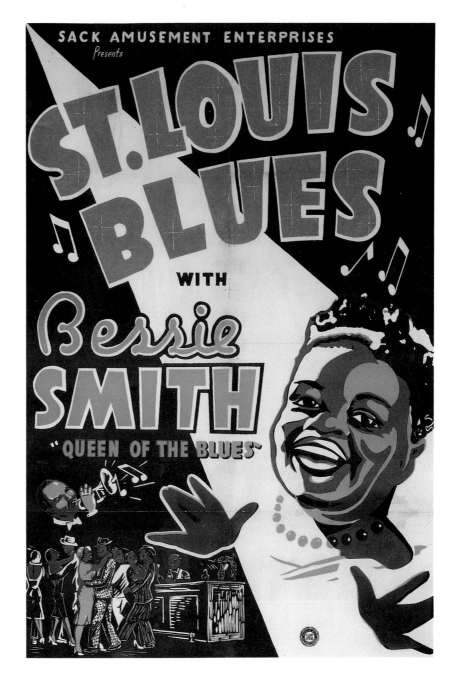

GIG AND SADDLE
1933
Goldberg Productions

A member of Al Capone's gang involved in a Chicago crap shoot once rubbed dice on jazz bandleader Lucius Leroy Millinder's back and parlayed $50 into $2,000, commenting, "You're a lucky guy." Lucky Millinder, as he became known, made several films later in the 1940s when he had the most popular band in Harlem. Some of the biggest names in jazz passed through his band, including Dizzy Gillespie, Harry Edison, Eddie "Lockjaw" Davis, Bill Doggett, Wynonie Harris, Bull Moose Jackson, and Sister Rosetta Tharpe. In this, Millinder's earliest film, he plays opposite Putney (no relation to Dorothy) Dandridge. The film was originally titled *Scandals of 1933*.

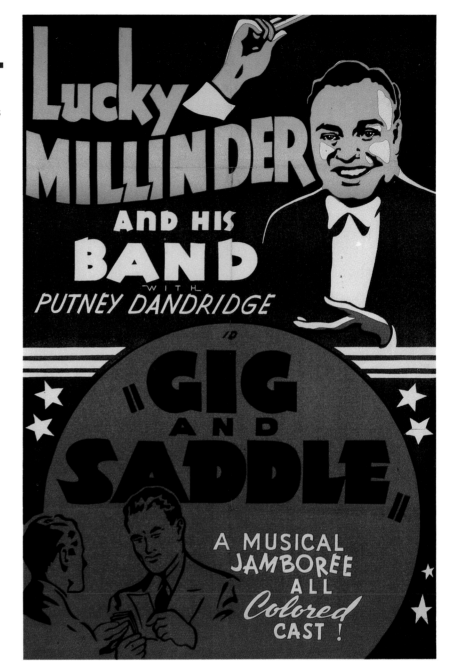

HARLEM IS HEAVEN
1932
Lincoln Productions

Not to be confused with the black-owned Lincoln Motion Picture Company of Los Angeles, Lincoln Productions, which was owned by whites and was located in New York City, made this as its first all-black film. It became a big moneymaker largely because of the drawing power of tap dancer Bill "Bojangles" Robinson, who, well into his fifties, had a smash-hit stage production of Lew Leslie's *Blackbirds* in 1928. Harlem was crazy for Bojangles. Eubie Blake, also a hit in vaudeville with his partner, Noble Sissle, makes an appearance at the piano. In spite of the film's title, the Harlem Renaissance had all but ended by this time.

REET-PETITE AND GONE
1947
Astor Pictures

The title refers to the comical jive that made Jordan a success. A few lines from the title song:

> I found a girl who beats them all, she isn't too short and isn't too tall.
> She's in the groove and right on the ball. She's reet, petite, and gone.
> Those other chicks leave me cold, you can't compare brass to 14k gold.
> After they made her they broke the mold. She's reet, petite, and gone.

A member of Chick Webb's orchestra, singing star June Richmond, plays opposite Jordan. Lorenzo Tucker, the "black Valentino," performs in his last featured screen role.

Louis Jordan's popularity came partially from the fact that between 1941 and 1946, Astor Pictures produced almost two dozen musical "soundies" (films played on a special type of jukebox that allowed one to both see and hear a performance) featuring his music.

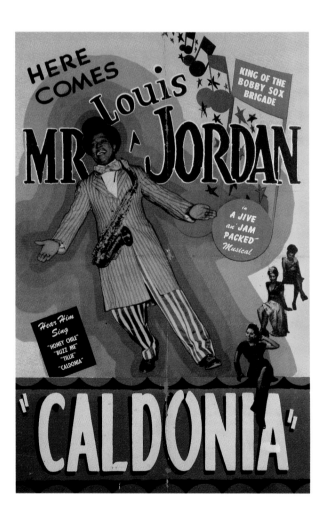

CALDONIA
1945
Astor Pictures

This eighteen-minute extended short became Louis Jordan's most famous. On the colorful poster Jordan wears a zoot suit with a "reet pleat and a drape shape" and carries his ever present saxophone. "Here comes Mr. 'Louis' Jordan" is a comical reference to the 1941 film Here Comes Mr. Jordan, in which Robert Montgomery plays a prizefighter and amateur saxophonist. Louis really swings in Caldonia, playing tenor sax instead of his usual alto. The enormous popularity of his band, the Tympany Five, was enough to lure black audiences into the segregated theaters where the film was shown.

BEWARE!
1946
Astor Pictures

Louis Jordan used this full-length musical romance in his climb to the top of the charts. By 1946 he had already had a dozen pop-chart hits, all million sellers. The title song, "Beware, Brother, Beware," was boycotted by women because of its comically sexist lyrics. Ultimately Jordan was forced to formally apologize in the lyrics of another song, "Look-Out Sister," released in 1947.

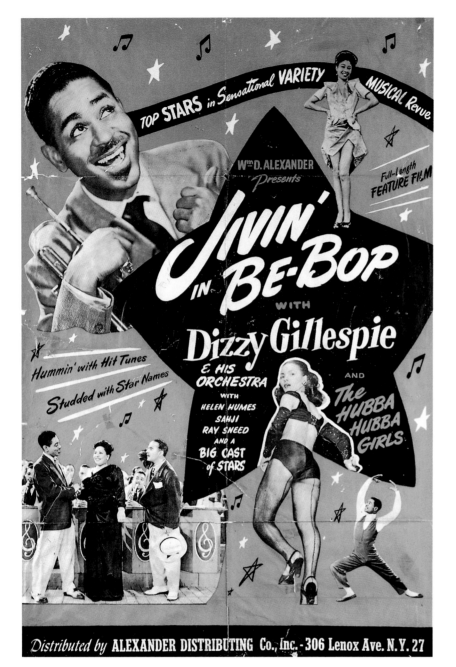

JIVIN' IN BE-BOP
1947
Alexander Productions
Courtesy of the Frank Newlin
Collection

Consisting simply of music and dancing, this film gave Dizzy Gillespie a chance to introduce his new bebop jazz style to movie audiences. The effort was not lacking in the talent department; in addition to Gillespie's singing, clowning, and trumpet showmanship, Helen Humes, James Moody, Milt Jackson, and Benny Carter performed "Oop Bop Sh'Bam," "Bob a Lee-ba," and "He Beeped When He Shoulda Bopped," among other tunes. Spencer Williams co-directed.

HI-DE-HO
1947
All-American News, Inc.

Cab Calloway's musical signature over the decades is a fitting title for this nine-minute musical short. Veteran musicians Doc Cheatham, Ben Webster, and Milt Hinton, among others, provided the music for Cab's "I Got a Right to Sing the Blues," "Hi-De-Ho Miracle Man," and "Frisco Flo." Calloway's significance in the history of black entertainment gives this little film a documentary value as well. In the 1930s and early 1940s his band contained some of the finest up-and-coming jazz legends, including Dizzy Gillespie, Chu Berry, Eddie Barefield, and Illinois Jacquet. When Calloway wasn't exploiting the idiom of scat singing with vocal novelties like "Minnie the Moocher," the band concentrated on jazz instrumentals which are highly regarded today. In 1971, going down a reception line at the White House during the Nixon administration, the President shook hands with Cab and said, "Mr. Ellington, it's so good that you're here. Pat and I just love your music."

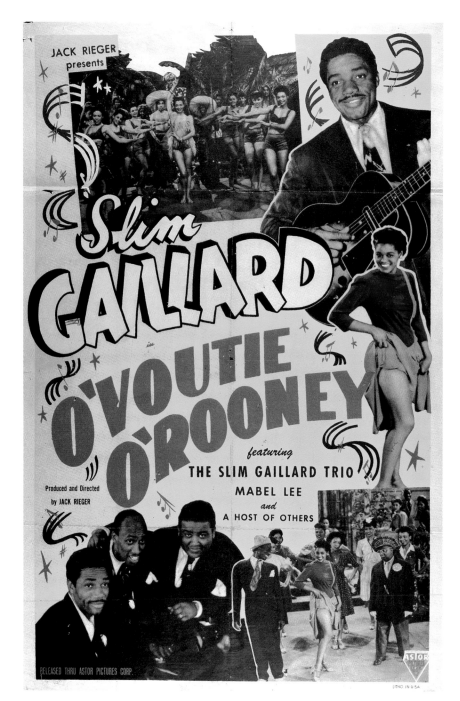

O'VOUTIE O'ROONEY
1947
Astor Pictures
Courtesy of the Bill Spicer
Collection

The title of this film comes as no surprise to anyone familiar with the work of guitarist Slim Gaillard, whose musical compositions include "Flat Foot Floogie," "Chili Beans Avoutie," and "Cement Mixer Putti Putti." Gaillard made a number of Hollywood features, such as *Hellzapoppin* (1941) and *Star Spangled Rhythm* (1942), but this was his only black-cast film.

**THE NAT "KING" COLE
MUSICAL STORY
1955
Universal-International
Roadshow**

The film traces Cole's rise to fame as a pianist. The son of a Chicago Protestant minister, he became a fixture in the jazz clubs on New York's Fifty-second Street. In the 1940s, when wartime spawned sentimentality, singers like Frank Sinatra, Perry Como, and Peggy Lee reached their largest audiences. The ballad was born, and Cole was a natural. Tall, dark, and incredibly suave, Cole became a "crossover" artist whose classy style appealed to white audiences as well. Cole's favorite tunes—"Pretend," "Route 66," "Sweet Lorraine," "Straighten Up and Fly Right," and "Darling, Je Vous Aime Beaucoup"—sold over a million copies each, making him the top black act in show business.

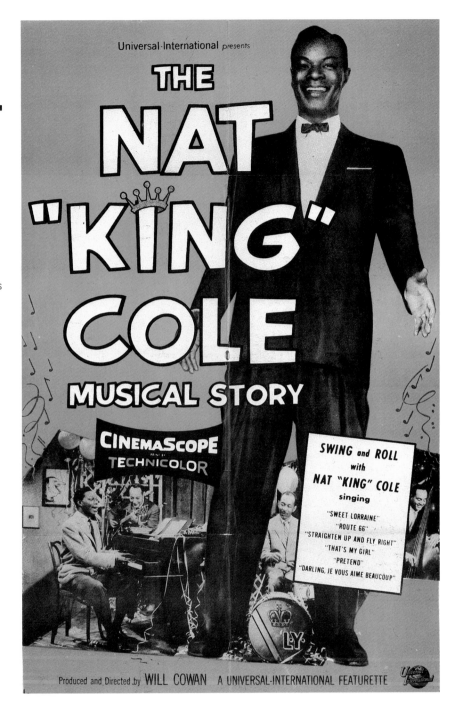

THE INTERNATIONAL SWEETHEARTS OF RHYTHM
1947
Associated Producers of Negro Motion Pictures

Modeled on the 1934 success of Ina Ray Hutton and her Melodears (an all-white female band), the International Sweethearts of Rhythm formed in 1937 at Piney Wood Ms. Country Life School for disadvantaged children. A multiracial band that included a Chinese-black saxophonist and a Mexican-black trumpeter, they were out of school and on their own by 1940. The white and mulatto members of the band had to wear dark makeup during tours of the South and were instructed to tell any suspicious sheriffs that their mothers were black. They also appeared in *That Man of Mine* (1947), which featured actress Ruby Dee at the start of her career. A thirty-minute documentary about this unusual group was released for public broadcast television in 1986.

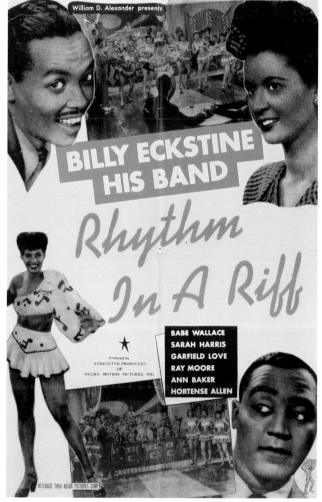

RHYTHM IN A RIFF
1947
Associated Producers of Negro Motion Pictures

"Mr. B," as Billy Eckstine was known, made this film when the advent of bebop and modern jazz broke up his phenomenal big band. It had included Dizzy Gillespie, Charlie Parker, Dexter Gordon, Lena Horne, Sarah Vaughan, Art Blakey, and Miles Davis, among other greats. M-G-M signed him to a solo recording contract in 1947, and he began his new guise as warm-voiced "balladeer." A few years and twelve Top 30 hits later, Eckstine turned down the male lead in 20th Century–Fox's *Carmen Jones* (1954) because he hated the demeaning "dems" and "dat" dialogue.

EBONY PARADE
1947
Astor Pictures

All-star musical compilations of previously released soundies were panoramic presentations of black stars for black audiences—Cab Calloway, Count Basie, the Mills Brothers, and other entertainers doing what they do best in an almost live-on-stage performance style. Mantan Moreland, as a magician, is used as a segue between each smash act. A decade before her phenomenal screen success, Dorothy Dandridge, with her name misspelled, is one of the youngest cast members.

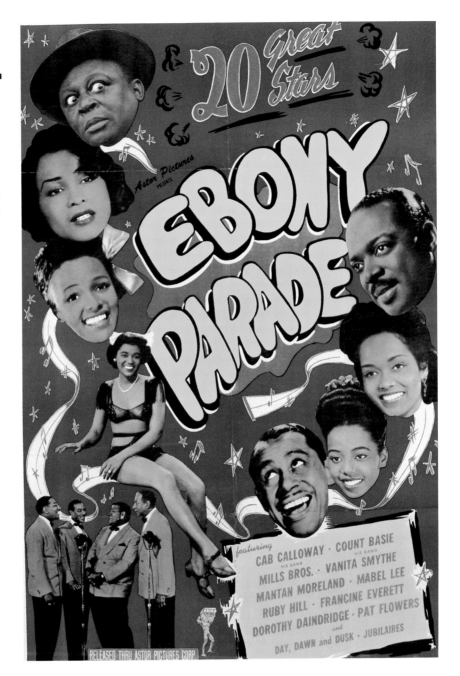

UNIVERSAL-INTERNATIONAL presents

"SUGAR CHILE"
ROBINSON

BILLIE
HOLIDAY

COUNT BASIE
and his SEXTET

Produced and Directed by
WILL COWAN
A UNIVERSAL-INTERNATIONAL FEATURETTE

Copyright 1951 by Universal Pictures Co., Inc.

"SUGAR CHILE" ROBINSON, BILLIE HOLIDAY, COUNT BASIE AND HIS SEXTET
1947
Universal-International
Courtesy of the Mitchell Diamond Collection

This fifteen-minute musical short is a virtual triptych of talent. In an extremely rare film appearance, "Lady Day" sings "God Bless the Child" and "Now, Baby, or Never." Count Basie swings out his all-time hit, "One O'Clock Jump," and "Sugar Chile" Robinson, a seven-year-old piano virtuoso, who had been thrust into the limelight with a role in the M-G-M Hollywood film *No Leave, No Love* (1946), plays and sings "Numbers Boogie" and "After School Boogie." In the 1950s while "Sugar Chile" was still being passed off as a child star, an adoring fan caught him smoking a cigar in his dressing room one night after he headlined a show at Harlem's Apollo Theater. The following day, the story in a local black newspaper ended his career in scandalous controversy at the age of seventeen.

ROCK 'N' ROLL REVUE
1955
Studio Films, Inc.

Another musical compilation of the world's finest musical and stage performers, this film was originally produced by Ben Frye for thirteen television episodes of *Harlem Variety Review*. It features Duke Ellington's "Take the 'A' Train," Lionel Hampton and his drumstick juggling, the Nat "King" Cole Trio, Honi Coles and his "high-speed rhythm" tap dancing, Ruth Brown, Dinah Washington's gutsy "Only a Moment Ago," and the Delta Rhythm Boys singing "When the Riffs That Trumpet Plays Are Groovy, You Know You're in Harlem."

RHYTHM AND BLUES REVUE
1955
Studio Films, Inc.

Onstage at Harlem's Apollo Theater, Willie Bryant hosts a cavalcade of musical greats. The Count Basie and Lionel Hampton bands jam, Bill Bailey (Pearl's tap-dancing brother) does Bojangles imitations, Nipsey Russell and Mantan Moreland provide vaudeville humor, and Joe Turner shouts the blues. Also featured are the Delta Rhythm Boys, Nat "King" Cole, Ruth Brown, Cab Calloway, Sarah Vaughan, Herb Jeffrey, and Amos Milburn in a unique all-black "all-star" musical film.

BLUES (L'INSPECTEUR CONNAIT LA MUSIQUE)
1955
Ciné Vog (France)
Courtesy of the Frank Newlin Collection

Sidney Bechet supplied the music and acted in this melodrama. The plot called for Bechet's character to be murdered with a clarinet. It's not clear whether it was fear of injury or respect for the clarinet that led Bechet to request that the actors "fake" the blow during the actual filming.

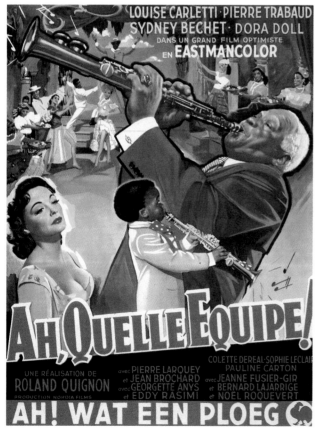

AH, QUELLE EQUIPE! (WHAT A TEAM!)
1956
Pathé Consortium (France)
Courtesy of the Michael Barson Collection

Very few Sidney Bechet fans have seen this rare comedy that cast him with a group of French variety performers. It was in stark contrast to *Série Noire* (1955), the gangster story Bechet made in France with Erich von Stroheim.

SATCHMO THE GREAT
1957
United Artists

Famed jazz icon Louis Armstrong's tour of Africa and Europe was recorded originally for an Edward R. Murrow CBS *See It Now* broadcast and later expanded as a documentary. The film was a far cry from the stereotypical antics this great artist was required to act out in Hollywood motion pictures. Among the songs performed were "Mack the Knife," "Indiana," and "Struttin' with Some Barbecue." Featured on the tour was W. C. Handy, who plays his all-time classic, "St. Louis Blues." Altogether, Armstrong appeared in more than fifty films.

DAS ERSTEMAL IM FILM
AMERIKAS BEKANNTESTER SCHAUSPIELER:
AL JOLSON
in
DER JAZZSÄNGER
DAS LIED DER VÄTER
REGIE: ALAN CROSLAND. IN DER WEIBLICHEN HAUPTROLLE: MAY MC AVOY
ALS TONFILMEINLAGE
UNTER ANDEREM
DER WELTBEKANNTE NEW-YORKER OBERKANTOR
JOSEF ROSENBLATT

FROM THE NECK UP: MINSTRELS

MODERN MINSTRELS
ca. 1930
A.D.W. Productions

A minstrel was a musician, singer, or comedian, usually Caucasian made up or "blacked up" as an African-American, presenting songs and jokes. Produced by the Woolever Brothers of Los Angeles, this minstrel comedy starred Cliff Nazzarro, a vaudeville master of ceremonies in all of the leading theaters in the late 1920s and early 1930s. Dubbed the "Master of Nonsense," Nazzarro originated a perplexing lingo known as "double talk," and perfected this routine so well that he was cast as "Swivel Tongue" in *You'll Never Get Rich* (1941) starring Fred Astaire.

THE JAZZ SINGER
1927
Warner Brothers
Courtesy of the Steve Shapiro Collection

Al Jolson in blackface was not the first choice for this landmark film. The role had been offered to George Jessel and Eddie Cantor, Jolson's peers. With a generous helping of blackface makeup, Jolson projected an unrealistic image of the black male as a big-lipped subservient, crooning "Mammy" on his knees. "Hap" Hadley, the poster's designer, was compensated by a declining Warner Bros. studio with stock shares rather than a salary. Hadley came out on top in that deal. (See page 106.)

A PAIR O' DICE
ca. 1930
A.D.W. Productions

The title of this minstrel-show film, another Woolever Brothers production, starring Lee "Bud" Harrison, makes a clever "play on words" illusion to Paradise. The poster displays a typically offensive Negro stereotype: two Pullman porters, on a break, kneeling in full uniform and shooting craps. Letting one's wages "ride" on a gamble is a consistent scenario for this kind of blackface humor.

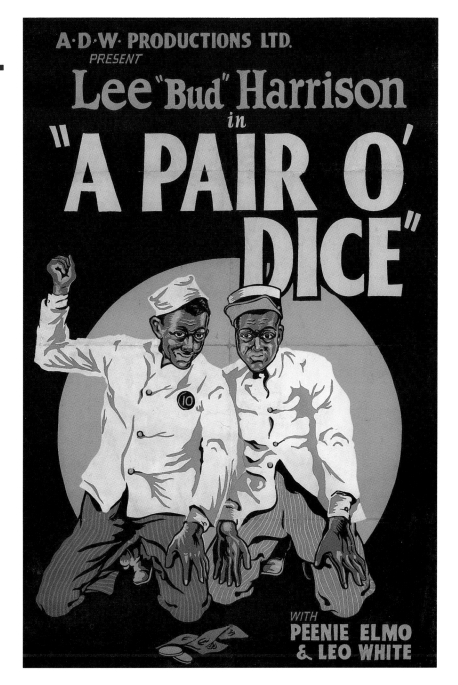

MINSTREL MAN
1944
P.R.C.

The title role was filled by Benny Fields, a white minstrel man and vaudeville performer in partnership with his wife, Blossom Seeley. The director, Joseph H. Lewis, subsequently directed the musical sequences for *The Jolson Story* (1946), another tribute to a blackface entertainer. In 1977, a black-cast film with the identical title brought a much needed perspective and dignity to the minstrel man.

HYPNOTIZED
1933
Son-Art World Wide Pictures

In 1929 Charles Mack and George Moran, the blackface minstrel comedy team better known as the Two Black Crows, split up due to financial differences. Mack took on Bert Swar as his new partner to make Paramount's *Anybody's War* (1930). It proved unsuccessful. Mack Sennett then offered the original Moran and Mack team a new contract to star in *Hypnotized*. Sadly, the techniques of Sennett, the "King of Silent Comedy Films," seemed out of sync in this sound film, in which Hattie McDaniel made one of her earliest appearances. Charles Mack died the following year in a car accident.

PINT-SIZED JESTERS

PART ELEVEN

THE CHAMPEEN
1923
Pathé

Considered one of the best episodes of the "Our Gang" series, this short film featured three-year-old Allen "Farina" Hoskins and Ernie "Sunshine Sammy" Morrison, who plays a fight promoter trying to raise money after he is caught stealing apples from a fruit stand. In a guilt-ridden fantasy sequence, Sammy is shown in prison stripes, chained and working on a rock pile under the watchful eye of an armed guard (white, of course). Ostensibly for a laugh, Hollywood persisted in damaging the self-image of the black child.

THREE MEN IN THE TUB
1938
Metro-Goldwyn-Mayer

Founded in 1922 by Hal Roach, the "Our Gang" series was so popular in the 1920s and 1930s that M-G-M acquired the rights and registered the name in 1938. The series continued until 1945, with deteriorating quality and revolving child actors playing similar roles. In the 1950s, it was sold to television under the name "Little Rascals" and viewers continued to enjoy the antics of these pint-sized jesters. In this romantic episode, Buckwheat (the black kids were named after cereals) had virtually no part in the plot. His real name was Billy Thomas, and after leaving the series he disappeared into show-business obscurity.

ALL'S FAIR
1938
Educational Films Corporation

This film, with a screenplay by Arthur Jarrett and Marcy Klauber, is from a series of comedies originally produced by Al Christie from 1934 to 1939. All one-"reelers," the series included *Pink Lemonade*, *Rhythm Saves the Day*, and *Way Down Yonder*, and featured the Cabin Kids, a harmonizing group of three boys and two girls, doing the things kids like to do best.

THE BISCUIT EATER
1940
Paramount Pictures
Courtesy of the Edward Mapp
Collection

Decades before Hollywood would risk the pairing of black and white men, it was willing to join black and white boys. This James Street story of a black boy and a white boy and their experience with a renegade dog was sufficiently popular to warrant a remake in 1972. In early Hollywood films, black characters were often given bizarre names as a means of deriding them. Thus, in *The Biscuit Eater*, Cordell Hickman is Text, Fred "Snowflake" Toones is 1st and 2nd Thessalonians, and Viola Davis is Aunt Charity.

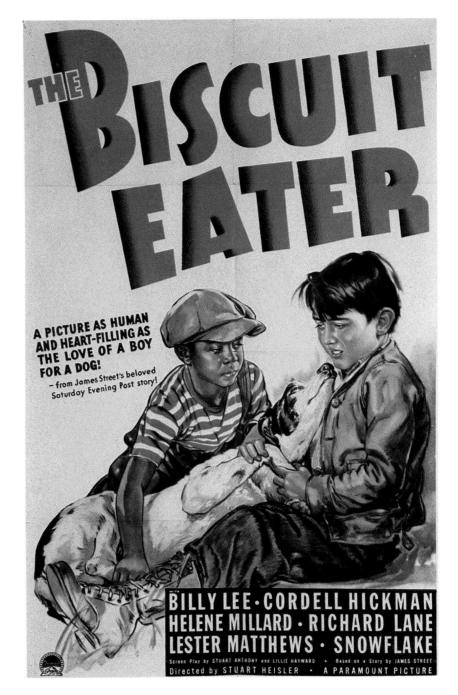

TAKE MY LIFE (MURDER RAP)
1941
Goldseal

The Dead End Kids/Bowery Boys, regulars on mainstream movie screens, were the prototype for the Harlem Dead End Kids of these two films. The plots were a thinly disguised bid to recruit black youths into the U.S. Army during the World War II era. With *Prison Bait*, Louise Beavers makes her second and last all-black-cast film. DeForest Covan, the lead "Tuff Kid," joined the Army before becoming a production manager for several Tarzan films. He returned to acting in Norwanda Pictures' all-black *No Time for Romance* (1948) and then appeared in *Carmen Jones* (1954) and *Pork Chop Hill* (1959), eventually becoming a regular on the television shows *Beulah*, *Amos 'n' Andy*, and *That's My Mama*.

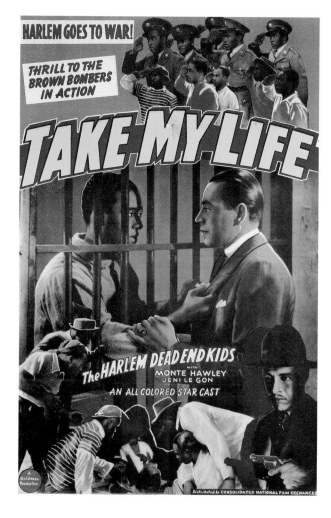

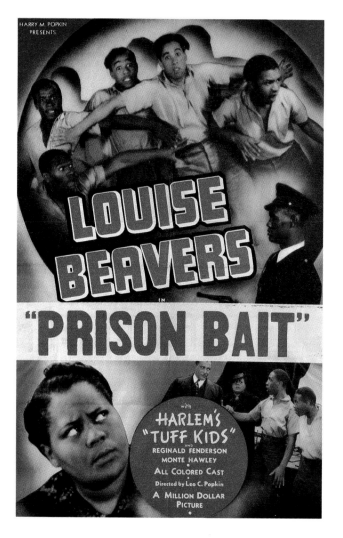

PRISON BAIT (REFORM SCHOOL)
1939
Million Dollar Pictures

TAKE A GIANT STEP
1960
United Artists

That black playwright Louis Peterson was signed to adapt his successful Broadway play into a screenplay was indeed rare in 1960. Even rarer was an American film concerned with the racial and sexual problems of black middle-class adolescents. Johnny Nash, a black pop singer, was an unconventional choice for the lead, a role which had served Lou Gossett better as the vehicle for his Broadway debut.

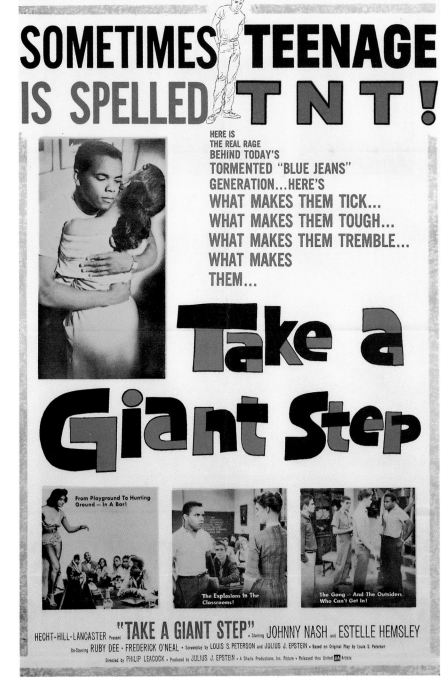

AFRICAN ATROCITY

PART TWELVE

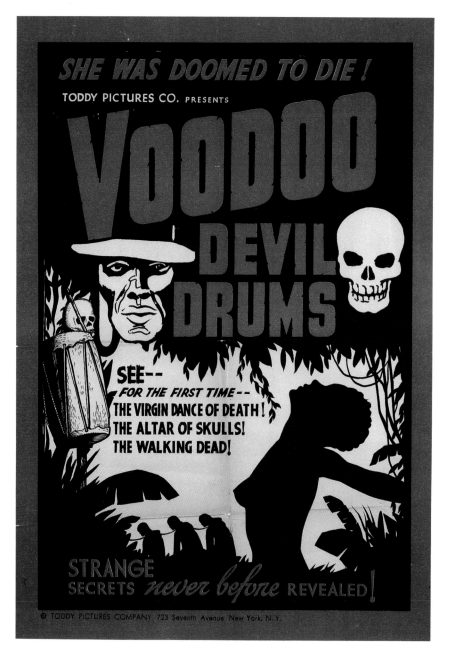

VOODOO DEVIL DRUMS
(VIRGIN BRIDES OF VOODOO)
ca. 1946
Toddy Pictures

This forty-four-minute semi-documentary offered a re-creation of voodoo rituals, black magic, and a resurrection of zombies in the search for rejuvenation. The film was frequently coupled with *Beast of Borneo* (ca. 1946). Toddy Pictures distributed them as a "2 Daring Pictures" exploitation package.

SHE DEVIL
1940
Louis Weiss Productions
Courtesy of the Glenn Bray
Collection

Adapted from *Drums O'Voodoo*, by the black dramatist J. Augustus Smith, who also starred with Laura Bowman and Abe Comathiere, the film examines the effect of primitive traditions on the lives of descendants of slaves in a small Louisiana town. Comathiere had played the title role in *The Black King* (1932). Bowman, ironically, had a "zombie phobia." In his biography of the actress, her husband, LeRoi Antoine, recalls a trip to Haiti during which Bowman was afraid she might die and be turned into a zombie. The film was also released under the titles *Voodoo Drums* (1933) and *Louisiana*.

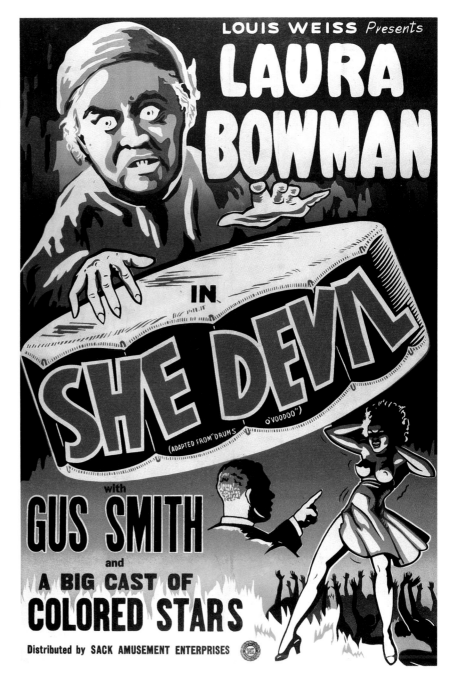

TARZAN'S PERIL
1951
RKO Radio Pictures

Of the many films in this series based on the Edgar Rice Burroughs character, this one is memorable for presenting a regal black African princess played by none other than Dorothy Dandridge, three years before her phenomenal success in the film *Carmen Jones*. Dandridge's great beauty gave dignity to what was otherwise a Hollywood stereotype.

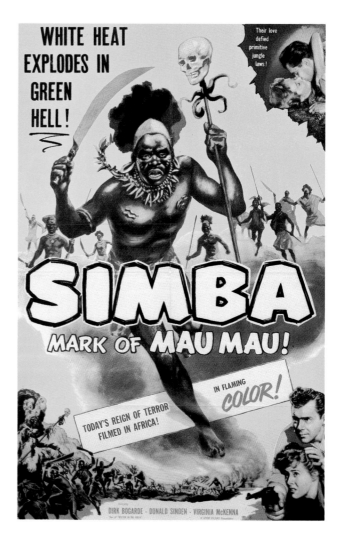

SIMBA
1955
J. Arthur Rank Productions (England)
Courtesy of the Edward Mapp Collection

The British filmed this semi-documentary of the Mau Mau movement in Kenya two years before the American studio M-G-M made the much publicized *Something of Value* (1957) on the same subject. Some of Britain's best black actors, including Earl Cameron and Orlando Martins, were in the cast. The poster's colorful depiction of the African as terrorist leaves little doubt as to where this film's sympathy lies.

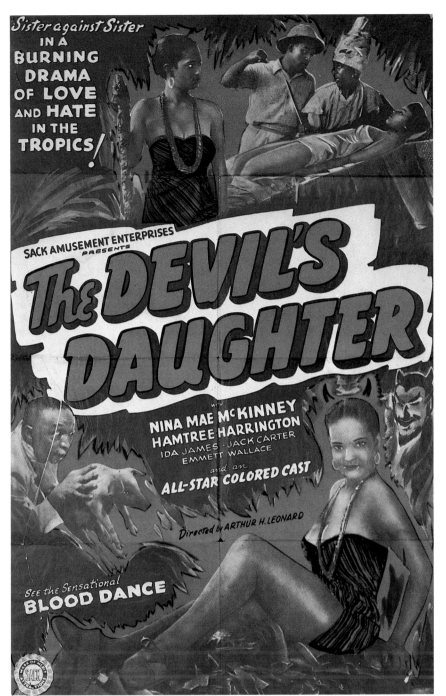

THE DEVIL'S DAUGHTER
1939
Goldberg Productions

Nina Mae McKinney, who was discovered in King Vidor's all-black musical *Hallelujah* (1929), enjoyed a modicum of success in several all-black dramas made by independent producers. Filmed on location in Jamaica, *The Devil's Daughter* allowed the "black Garbo," as McKinney was sometimes billed, to play an exotic in the flashiest of her films. McKinney's career never really took off, because Hollywood was not yet willing to accept a black leading lady. The film's "blood dance" was a typical ploy to attract sensation seekers.

MAU-MAU
1950s
Rock-Price Productions

That the Mau Mau killed few whites but thousands of their fellow Kikuyus is belied by the sensationalism of this film's poster. Immediately following the initial Mau Mau rebellion, moviemakers raced to be the first with their films on the topic. Filmed in Kenya, *Mau-Mau* reconstructs the Mau Mau initiation ceremony as well as scenes of massacres.

THE MARK OF THE HAWK
1958
Universal-International
Courtesy of the Edward Mapp Collection

Filmed in eastern Nigeria (Biafra) and funded by the Presbyterian Church, this film is about a labor movement in Africa, and is imbued with strong religious overtones. The church wanted to show the world the good work it was doing. Sidney Poitier plays an African leader who supports colonialism; as Poitier's wife, Eartha Kitt has little to do but chant "This Man Is Mine," the theme song.

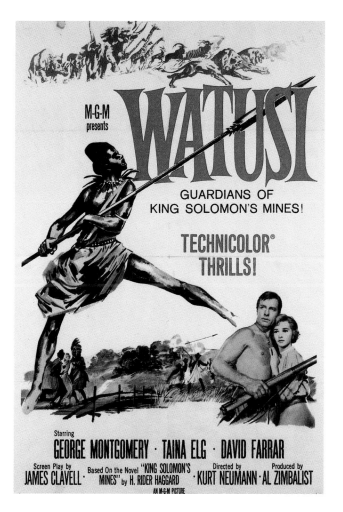

WATUSI
1959
Metro-Goldwyn-Mayer

In this remake of H. Rider Haggard's *King Solomon's Mines*, Rex Ingram plays Umbopa, a role that Paul Robeson had accepted with reluctance in the 1937 British film version. Although his career was declining, Ingram made a convincing Watusi with his tall stature; he was certainly no stranger to African characterizations. The film utilized excess jungle footage from *King Solomon's Mines* (1950).

UPTOWN SATURDAY NIGHT: RACE FILMS

PART THIRTEEN

THE PEANUT MAN
1947
Consolidated Pictures

Anyone familiar with black history would readily connect this film title with Dr. George Washington Carver. Carver is portrayed by Clarence Muse, a former member of the famed Lafayette Players and the composer of the song "When It's Sleepy Time Down South." Almost all of the black-cast films of the 1930s and 1940s were shot in black and white, although the posters that advertised them were extremely colorful. This film was shot in color, a rarity.

THE BLACK KING
(HARLEM HOT SHOT)
1932
Southland Pictures

One of the earliest films to focus on the "Back to Africa" movement, *The Black King* was billed as a satire on the life of Marcus Garvey. Made by an independent white-owned company, the film forced the actors to speak in stereotypical black English, thereby ridiculing the notion of a black king. Sued for outstanding debts, Southland Pictures did not make any more films. (See page 128.)

BROKEN STRINGS
1940
International Roadshows
Courtesy of the Edward Mapp Collection

Clarence Muse starred in and co-wrote the screenplay for this independently made all-black drama. His role as a dignified professional concert violinist is perhaps his finest and far from the Hollywood servant types that he was known for. Featured in this film, although not credited in the poster, is Matthew Beard, better known as Stymie from the popular "Our Gang" comedy series.

THE BROKEN EARTH
1939
Sack Amusement Enterprises

Clarence Muse had an uncanny ability to breathe realism and spirituality into his characterizations of the down-home rural family men he had been playing since *Hearts in Dixie* (1929). In this short film, Muse is musically supported by Frieda Shaw's Choir singing the spirituals "All God's Chillun Got Shoes" and "Swing Low, Sweet Chariot." The cinematographer's effective use of natural light gave the scenes the look of a painterly landscape masterpiece. *The Broken Earth* is one of the film treasures discovered in a Tyler, Texas, warehouse in 1983.

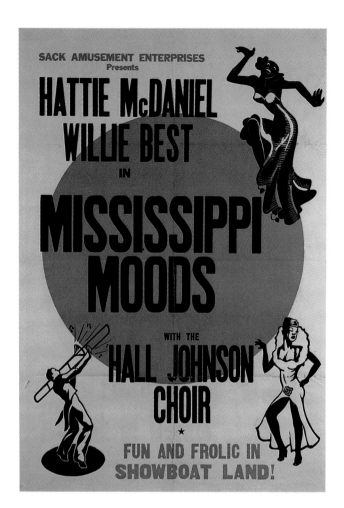

MISSISSIPPI MOODS
ca. 1940
Sack Amusement Enterprises

Hattie McDaniel and Willie Best would be reunited for an all-black musical sequence in the 1943 all-star *Thank Your Lucky Stars* for Warner Bros. Like so many race films, *Mississippi Moods* is totally unknown to the mainstream movie industry. The film is not even mentioned in *Hattie*, the 1990 biography of McDaniel.

SWANEE SHOWBOAT
1940
Ajax Pictures

In this little-known feature, McKinney, billed as Nina, is presented as a true "colored" beauty in a pose that would later be associated with Betty Grable on her classic World War II pinup. The river showboat of the title is the stage for the antics of musicians and comedians.

DEEP SOUTH
1930
Sack Amusement Enterprises

In his early Hollywood films, Willie Best was billed as "Sleep 'n' Eat." His comedic style and timing was reminiscent of that of Stepin Fetchit. Primarily a character actor, Best received star billing in this race movie. Clarence Muse, who had just won acclaim in the role of Nappus in *Hearts in Dixie* (1929), lends able support in this film.

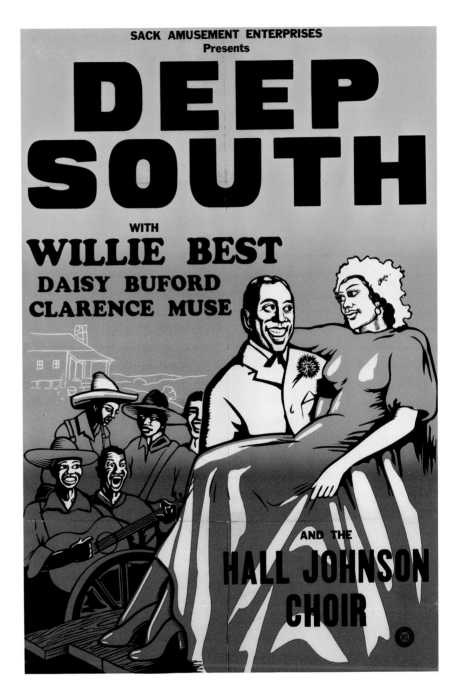

MIDNIGHT MENACE
1946
All-American News, Inc.

These three shorts starring ladies' man Lollypop Jones featured mystery, mayhem, and music. The cast was unknown except for Sybyl Lewis, who had already been on the race-movie circuit, appearing in *Mystery in Swing* (1938), *Broken Strings* (1940), and *Am I Guilty?* (1940).

CHICAGO AFTER DARK
1946
All-American News, Inc.

LUCKY GAMBLERS
1946
All-American News, Inc.

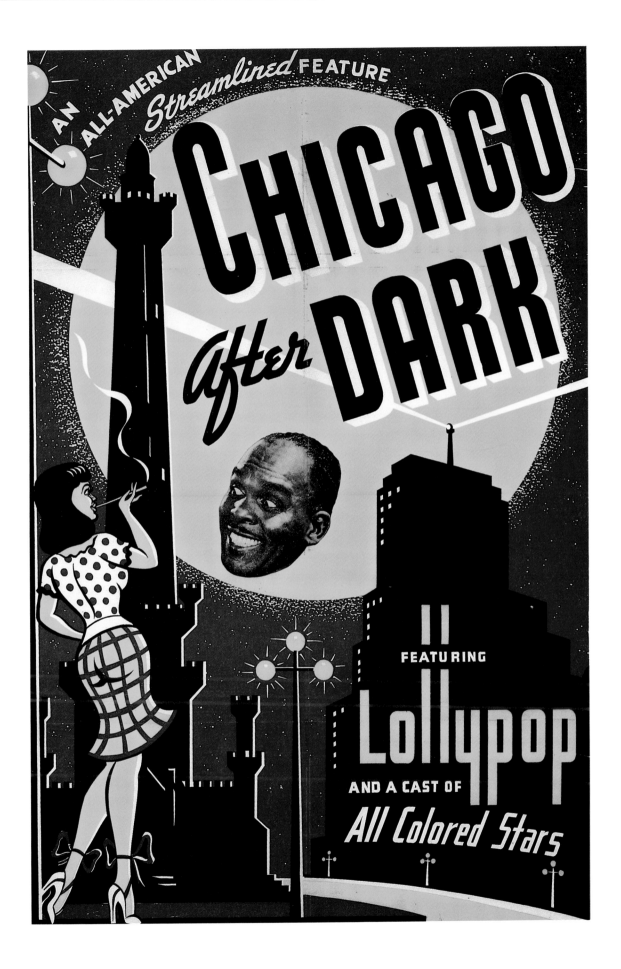

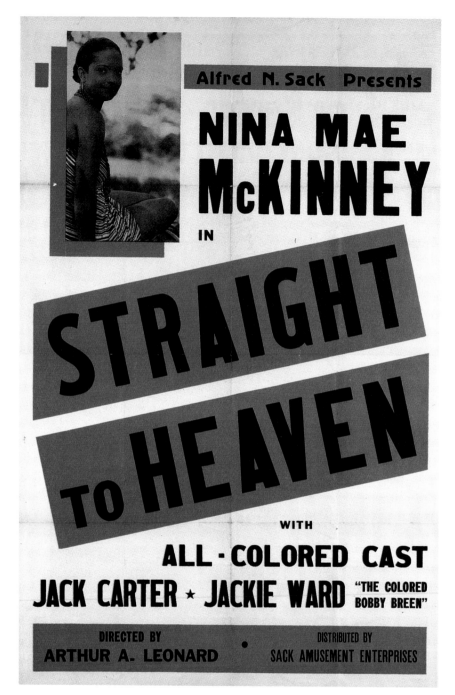

STRAIGHT TO HEAVEN
1939
Million Dollar Pictures

Parallel to the Cagney, Bogart, and Raft gangster melodramas emerging from Hollywood in the 1930s were films about syndicate crime in the black community. To carry the parallel even further, a young boy singer, Jackie Ward, is billed as "the colored Bobby Breen." Breen was a white teenage "singing sensation" of several mainstream films of this era. An aged and overweight Lorenzo Tucker, no longer displaying the "black Valentino" romantic look that made him so famous in his days with Oscar Micheaux, here plays an amoral, gum-chewing hit man who kidnaps Nina Mae McKinney as part of a scandal involving a canned-food distributor in Harlem.

GANG SMASHERS (GUN MOLL)
1938
Million Dollar Pictures

During the Depression years, black audiences sought temporary refuge from their troubles in segregated theaters showing films with escapist themes, such as this one starring Nina Mae McKinney as a dame who runs Harlem's underworld rackets. Although he often starred in films of this genre, Ralph Cooper chose to write the screenplay for this one instead.

RACKET DOCTOR (AM I GUILTY?)
1940
Supreme Pictures/Toddy Pictures

Tired of playing gangster roles in race films, Ralph Cooper quit Million Dollar Pictures in 1939 (he was one of its original founders) and joined Supreme Pictures to make this film. Not devoted exclusively to making black-cast films, Supreme was noted for a series of Western movies with Johnny Mack Brown and Bob Steele. Lending support to Cooper in *Racket Doctor* are Sam McDaniel (Hattie's brother) and Marcella Moreland (Mantan's daughter).

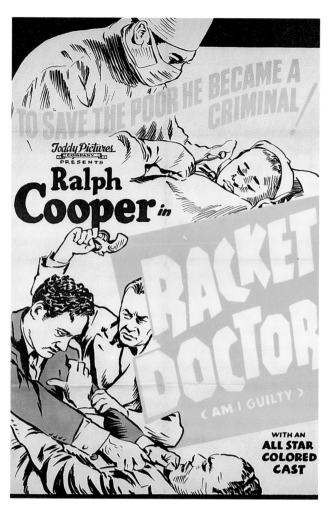

GANGSTERS ON THE LOOSE
1937
Million Dollar Pictures

A triple-threat man, Ralph Cooper wrote the original story and the screenplay and starred in this movie, which has been re-released as *Bargain with Bullets*. Theresa Harris gained recognition as Eddie "Rochester" Anderson's number one girlfriend in several Jack Benny movies. Les Hite's Cotton Club band, featuring Eddie Barefield's saxophone, provides musical interludes to lighten the underworld drama.

POLICY MAN
1938
Creative Cinema Corp.

Black audiences were acquainted with "numbers runners" policy men from the seedy sides of Harlem's gambling underworld. This was an early role for James Baskett, the star who nine years later would appear as Uncle Remus in Walt Disney's live-action animated film *Song of the South* (1947). *Policy Man* also marks the first screen appearance of Count Basie and his orchestra, including Herschel Evans, Lester Young, Buck Clayton, Dicky Wells, and the most famous rhythm section in jazz history, Walter Page, Freddie Green, and Joe Jones.

FOUR SHALL DIE
1940
Million Dollar Pictures

At the age of seventeen, Dorothy Dandridge made her first appearance in an all-black-cast film, one of the many in which Mantan Moreland, the comedian, starred. During this time, Dandridge was singing in nightclubs with her sister Vivian and another performer, Etta Jones. The act was billed as the Dandridge Sisters. The film was rereleased under the title *Condemned Men* in 1946.

DOUBLE DEAL
1939
International Roadshows

Monte Hawley, the film's leading man, was compared variously to Clark Gable and George Raft because of his rugged good looks and his ability to play "tough guys" in a smooth manner. Jeni Le Gon, his leading lady, had made her screen debut earlier opposite Bill "Bojangles" Robinson in RKO's *Hooray for Love* (1935). Shelton Brooks, composer of the hits "Darktown Strutters Ball" and "Some of These Days," appeared as himself in one scene; he also contributed two songs to the film's score.

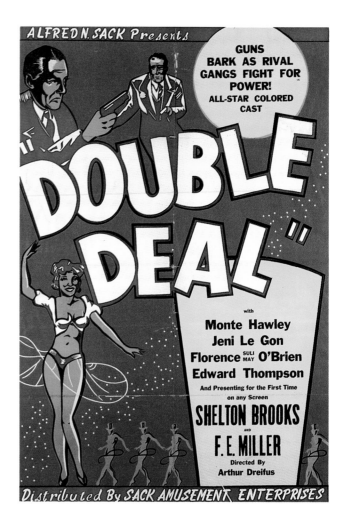

MOON OVER HARLEM
1939
Meteor Productions, Inc.

Noted jazz clarinetist Sidney Bechet and his real-life wife, Marieluise, are part of the cast, which features twenty chorus girls, a choir of forty-six voices, and a sixty-piece symphony orchestra under the musical direction of Donald Heywood. Oddly enough, all of the music provided is only background for a tale of the numbers racket in Harlem's underworld. Born in New Orleans in 1897, Bechet began his career at the age of eleven, playing with jazz greats Bunk Johnson, Freddie Keppard, and King Oliver. Constantly touring America and Europe in the 1920s, he performed with Mistinguett, the queen of French music halls, and accompanied Josephine Baker in *La Revue Nègre*. By the 1930s the popularity of his heavy vibrato Creole sound on the clarinet and the soprano saxophone became eclipsed by the rapidly emerging Big Band sound. He opened up a tailor shop in Harlem to make ends meet until 1938, when the seminal "Panassie" recording sessions with Tommy Ladnier, Mezz Mezzrow, and James P. Johnson spearheaded a national resurgence of New Orleans' "Storyville" jazz. Bechet became an expatriate in 1942, spending the rest of his life in Paris. Profoundly influential and as popular as Edith Piaf, he made several films in Paris in the 1950s.

LIFE GOES ON (HIS HARLEM WIFE)
1938
Million Dollar Pictures
Courtesy of the Glenn Bray Collection

The first of the two all-black-cast films made by the gifted actress Louise Beavers, the courtroom drama *Life Goes On* dealt with the joys and frustrations of a widow as a single parent. Beavers is ably supported by Edward Thompson, an alumnus of Harlem's famous Lafayette Players Stock Company, and Reginald Fenderson, a race-movie regular, as her two sons. Thompson plays an attorney who defends Fenderson, his brother, after he is unjustly accused of murder.

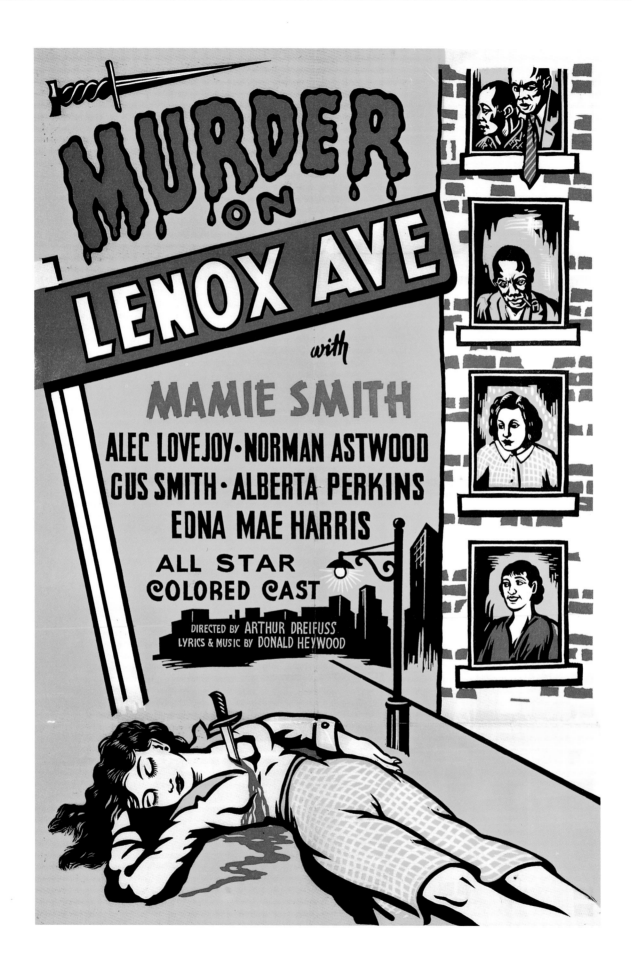

MURDER ON LENOX AVE
1941
Colonnade Pictures

The film follows the tangled lives of the various tenants of a Harlem brownstone. Chorus girls, musicians, quiet families, and criminals live side by side and involve each other in heartbreak tragedy. Donald Heywood and his orchestra provided the music for a cabaret setting, offering a suitable backdrop for the requisite song-and-dance numbers. Already a well-known blues singer, Mamie Smith sings one song.

PARADISE IN HARLEM
1939
Jubilee Pictures Corporation

Originally titled *Othello in Harlem*, this film features many of the names associated with race movies, including Mamie Smith, Edna Mae Harris, Francine Everett, and Juanita Hall, the diminutive diva who would later become a hit on Broadway as Bloody Mary in *South Pacific*. Mixing jazz and gangsters, the film is set in a barroom cabaret, where Lucky Millinder and his orchestra, with Mamie Smith, beat out "Harlem Serenade," "Harlem Blues," and "Why Have You Left Me Blue?"

MIRACLE IN HARLEM
1948
Herald Pictures

Produced by Jack and David Goldberg, one of the last race movies of the independent film movement. A murder mystery centering on a family-owned candy business, *Miracle in Harlem* takes a serious look at post–World War II black America prior to the advent of Hollywood's "Negro problem" films of the 1950s. Sheila Guyse sings a very spiritual rendition of "Look Down That Lonesome Road," and the Broadway singer Juanita Hall belts out "Chocolate Candy Blues." William Greaves, who plays the heroine's boyfriend, later became an independent producer/director. He is perhaps best known as the executive producer of Richard Pryor's *Bustin' Loose* (1981).

SUNDAY SINNERS
1940
Goldberg Productions

SUNDAY SINNERS
1940
Goldberg Productions
Courtesy of the Glenn Bray Collection

Like so many other films in the race genre, *Sunday Sinners* concentrated on the eternal conflict between good and evil, in this case between the church pulpit and street racketeers. Donald Heywood, a prominent composer for black-cast films since the early 1930s, wrote the tunes for Mamie Smith (wife of the producer Jack Goldberg) to sing in this movie after she had disbanded her orchestra, the Jazz Hounds. The film includes a deplorable stereotypical characterization of a Chinese laundryman, which in a "race film" is the ultimate irony.

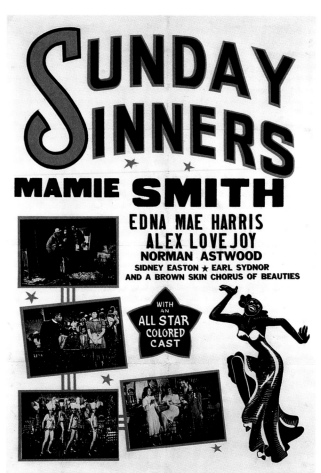

SOULS OF SIN
1949
Alexander Productions

Competition from Hollywood in the form of problem films, including *Home of the Brave* (1949) and *Lost Boundaries* (1949), brought a cessation of activity by black independent producers like William D. Alexander. *Souls of Sin* is considered to be the last race movie made by a black producer. Glamour girl singer Savannah Churchill plays Regina, the siren who leads the film's male star, Dollar Bill, played by Jimmy Wright, to his inevitable destruction. Best known for her famous recording "I Want to Be Loved by Only You," Churchill introduces in this film her newest hit, "The Things You Do to Me," written in collaboration with King Records' Henry Glover. Wright is a veteran of several Broadway productions, including *Mamba's Daughters* and *Walk Together, Children.*

WILLIAM D.
ALEXANDER
presents

SOULS OF SIN

SAVANNAH CHURCHILL
JIMMY WRIGHT

EMORY RICHARDSON
BILLIE ALLEN
WILLIAM GREAVES
SCOTT & HARRIS
Written & Directed by Powell Lindsay

WITH A VOICE: THE POSTWAR PERIOD

PART FOURTEEN

HOME OF THE BRAVE
1949
United Artists
Courtesy of the Edward Mapp Collection

Based on a Broadway play about anti-Semitism, the film focused instead on racism directed against blacks in World War II. James Edwards gave a sensitive and emotionally charged performance as Private Moss, who suffers more abuse from his fellow soldiers than from the enemy. A forerunner of similar "problem" films, the production was undertaken in secrecy by Stanley Kramer, who was to produce *The Defiant Ones*, a decade later.

WITHOUT PITY (SENZA PIETÀ)
1948
Lux Films, Inc. (Italy)

Produced by Carlo Ponti and scripted by Federico Fellini, this bilingual (English-Italian) film deals with the friendship between a black American Army sergeant (John Kitzmiller) and a homeless Italian girl (Carla Del Poggio) set in the black-market area of the Leghorn waterfront during the postwar occupation of Italy. In his preliminary research, Fellini resorted to disguises in order to penetrate the postwar underworld. Passing himself off as a returned prisoner of war and "ready for anything," Fellini settled near the docks in an old boardinghouse and went along with hijacking gangs to loot supply depots. Kitzmiller became Italy's leading actor in post–World War II Italian cinema. *Without Pity* was probably the most widely distributed of his more than forty films. He died in 1965 in Rome without ever becoming known to black American movie audiences.

ANGELO
1951
Scalera Productions (Italy)

After World War II, cinéma vérité films came to the fore, bringing many Italian-made motion pictures to American audiences. Frequently they explored the effects of an American occupation army that included blacks on the lives of the Europeans it liberated. Angelo, a five-year-old mulatto child, born to an Italian mother and a black father, is not easily accepted by the other children in his village.

LOST BOUNDARIES
1949
Film Classics, Inc.
Courtesy of the Edward Mapp Collection

The second film in a single year to deal with the issue of "passing" was a dramatization of a true story in *Reader's Digest*. As with *Pinky* (1949), the black characters are portrayed by white actors. However, two black performers are cast in minor roles. Veteran actor Canada Lee and a very young William Greaves lend a definitive authenticity to this semi-documentary as, respectively, a Harlem police officer and a college student.

NATIVE SON
1951
Classic Pictures

Richard Wright was unable to obtain a Hollywood company's financing for the film version of his classic novel; he was forced to film in Argentina and intercut scenes of the slums on Chicago's South Side. Wright, who was forty-three at the time, attempted unconvincingly to play a twenty-year-old Bigger Thomas, the hardened chauffeur whose hopeless life takes a tragic turn when he unintentionally kills a white woman. Ultimately, the film was an artistic and financial failure.

I PASSED FOR WHITE
1960
Allied Artists

During the era of the double feature, theaters would show an "A" main attraction and a "B" secondary filler movie. These low-budget potboilers frequently involved actors of untested or limited abilities. Their posters usually avoided graphic design in favor of photographs of actors in suggestive poses accompanied by risqué captions. This film tells of the desperate plight of a white-skinned black woman who decides to pass for white when she falls in love with the handsome young scion of a wealthy socialite family.

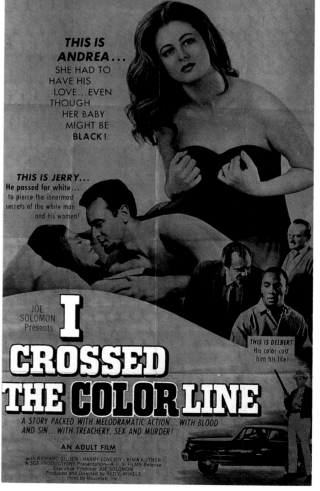

I CROSSED THE COLOR LINE
1966
U.S. Films

Not since 1915 had there been a film about the vicious and secret Ku Klux Klan. All of the major Hollywood studios had stories on the Klan, but because of pressure from various elements, particularly in the South, none had touched the explosive theme as in this film. Richard Gilden was a veteran of television's *Gunsmoke*, *Rawhide*, and *Playhouse 90*. Though he was light-skinned, he spent many hours with makeup men to make it believable that his character could change his appearance and pass for white in order to join the Klan and avenge the killing of his little daughter.

THE WORLD, THE FLESH, AND THE DEVIL
1959
Metro-Goldwyn-Mayer
Courtesy of the Edward Mapp Collection

The poster for this slightly offbeat film promised more than was actually delivered. Adding a new twist to the eternal triangle, the plot starred Harry Belafonte in a sexually neutralized role. He is one of three people to survive a nuclear war. Obviously, the other two are a white woman and a white man. The movie is an embodiment of the liberal ideology of the period and its optimistic finale is a metaphor for a world yet to come.

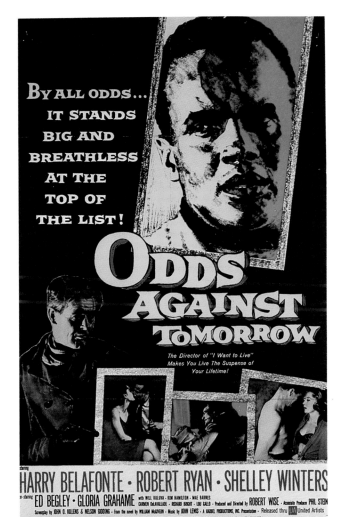

ODDS AGAINST TOMORROW
1959
United Artists

Among this film's distinctions are a taut script with emotionally explosive dialogue. Though black novelist John Oliver Killens was credited with the writing of the film, it was actually the work of Abraham Polonsky, who was blacklisted at the time. The instant recognition attached to the Belafonte name did surprisingly little to save this unsuccessful film about racist hatred among three bank robbers. A brief but promising performance is given by Cicely Tyson as a nightclub girl, and dancer Carmen De Lavallade makes a very sleek appearance as a Belafonte girlfriend.

IT WON'T RUB OFF, BABY!
(SWEET LOVE, BITTER)
1967
Film 2 Associates
Courtesy of the Edward Mapp Collection

Based on the novel *Night Song* by John Williams, a noted black writer, the film features comedian Dick Gregory in his only film. Considered a thinly disguised portrait of Charlie "Bird" Parker, the film is still shown at jazz film festivals because of its unique look and sound. In 1967, Robert Hooks also co-founded the renowned Negro Ensemble Company on Broadway.

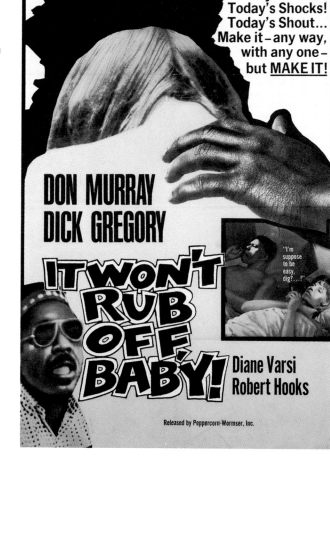

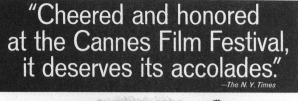

ONE POTATO, TWO POTATO
1964
Bawalco Picture Company

Films had presented glimpses of interracial romance before, but this was the first screen study of interracial marriage. One American film festival rejected it because it contained a scene in which the white star and her black counterpart kiss. Acclaimed abroad for its cynical and realistic look at black America, the film did not receive wide distribution in the United States. Bernie Hamilton gave his finest screen performance as a responsible, sensitive, and intelligent black man.

NOTHING BUT A MAN
1963
Cinema V
Courtesy of the Edward Mapp Collection

This low-budget independently produced film about life in segregated rural Alabama from a black perspective is widely regarded as one of the finest films ever made about black family life. Though it was highly praised at the New York Film Festival, its commercial success was limited due to its distributor's doubts about its potential as a moneymaker. The African-American character seeks to be "nothing but a man" in American society—a subject that is rarely explored in commercial films.

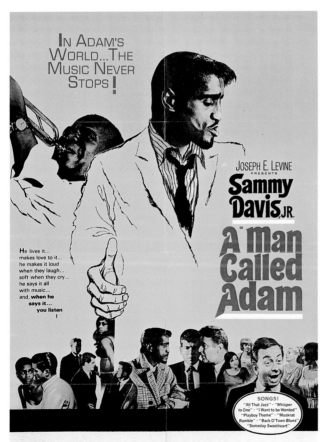

A MAN CALLED ADAM
1966
Embassy Pictures

Sammy Davis, Jr., stars as a troubled jazz trumpeter (ghosted by Nat Adderley) who finds himself unable to cope with the problems of everyday life in New York City. Louis Armstrong lends authenticity in the role of aging trumpeter Willie "Sweet Daddy" Ferguson, who is trying to make a comeback from retirement. The musicians Benny Carter, Kai Winding, and Nat Adderley, among others, are featured. Mel Tormé sings "All That Jazz." A similar theme was explored in later films such as *Round Midnight* (1986).

NO WAY OUT
1950
20th Century–Fox
Courtesy of the Edward Mapp
Collection

This film marks the debut of Sidney Poitier in the role of a saintly noble Negro doctor, the first of a series of similar characters he was to bring to the screen. Poitier's only previous film experience was in a documentary, *From Whence Cometh My Help* (1949). Set in a hospital, the plot centers on the death of a white gangster which causes riots in the ghetto. Though the script was nominated for an Academy Award, critics panned the production as being designed solely for the purposes of agitation and propaganda, unworthy of cinematic consideration. The American poster displays the distinctive design of Saul Bass.

CRY, THE BELOVED COUNTRY
1952
United Artists

Canada Lee gave his best screen performance in this, his final film. In his second role, Sidney Poitier played a young African priest. Since the movie was made in apartheid South Africa, both Lee and Poitier were required to enter the country as laborers indentured to Zoltan Korda, the film's white producer/director. Under the title *African Fury*, one poster tries to exploit the racial issue. Neither poster prominently displays a visual image of Canada Lee, although he is the film's star.

AFRICAN FURY
(CRY, THE BELOVED COUNTRY)
1952
United Artists

LILIES OF THE FIELD
1963
United Artists

Becoming the first black male in history to win the coveted prize for best actor, Sidney Poitier took home an Academy Award for his portrayal of an informal acolyte for a group of German nuns. Significantly, this role was politically more acceptable to the mass white audiences than his previous gritty and harder-edged performances in *The Defiant Ones* (1958) and *A Raisin in the Sun* (1961). The film's director, Ralph Nelson, financed the production with his home as collateral and shot the script in fourteen days. Other titles considered for the film were *Piety in the Sky*, *The Amen Man*, and *The Mischief Maker*.

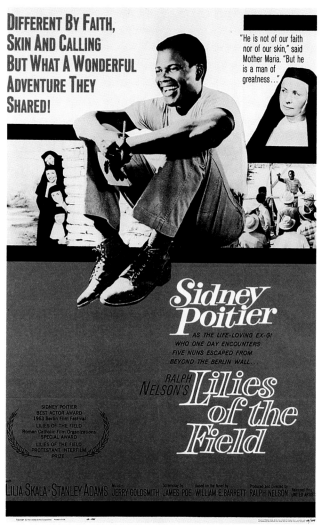

A RAISIN IN THE SUN
1961
Columbia Pictures

Lorraine Hansberry drew the title of her prize-winning play from the Langston Hughes poem "What Happens to a Dream Deferred?" Although many directors, including Elia Kazan and Otto Preminger, received overtures to direct this film, Lloyd Richards, the black director who had received critical acclaim for his direction of the award-winning play, was never even approached by producer David Susskind. The film was selected as the official U.S. entry in the Cannes Film Festival. Note the "sole above the title billing," for the first time for Poitier, who now had proven his ability to carry a film to box-office success.

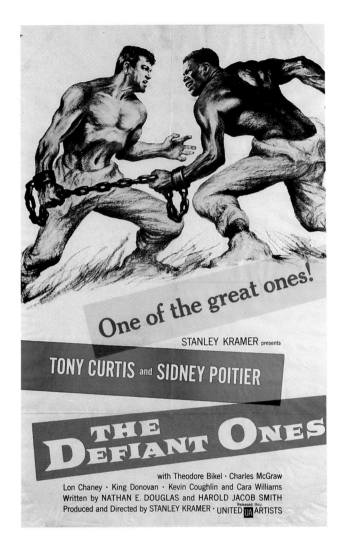

THE DEFIANT ONES
1958
United Artists

This groundbreaking film gave Poitier his first opportunity to co-star and receive top cast billing. He won the best actor award at the Berlin Film Festival for what is said to be the most physically demanding role of his career. Director Stanley Kramer was voted best director by the New York Film Critics for his treatment of the theme of interracial brotherhood. Ivan Dixon, then an unknown bit player, served as Poitier's stand-in during the several weeks of shooting in extreme weather conditions.

GUESS WHO'S COMING TO DINNER
1967
Columbia Pictures

Along with his *Home of the Brave* (1949) and *The Defiant Ones* (1958), this film was irrefutable evidence of producer Stanley Kramer's consistent commitment to racial understanding. Footage of Poitier's interracial love scenes was left on the cutting-room floor, and audiences were allowed only one fleeting kiss glimpsed in a taxi's rearview mirror during the opening credits. Nonetheless, the film broke box-office records and Poitier was voted most popular male star by the Theater Owners of America.

What started out as a tribute to Louis Jordan on my dorm-room wall during my bawdy days at Bard College eventually became my compulsion. This book attests to my twenty years of hunger for this exceedingly special art form.

Unlike the more famous black Hollywood movie posters, posters for independently produced black titles were often printed with little to nonexistent budgets, resulting in artwork that is, in many cases, more interesting than the film itself. The simple design, brilliant color, and stylized humor throughout make them icons, both of history and of art. Though many of the original all-black-cast films have been lost or destroyed or have just disintegrated, conservation efforts by film archives possessing existing footage are constantly under way.

The number of films available on video is growing, but they are not necessarily easy to find. Ask your local or a specialized video store for assistance. They will also be able to direct you to mail-order video companies. From time to time, some of the films are shown on television as well.

I would like to acknowledge the many people who have made this book what it is. First, those friends and collectors who share this obsession, and some who were kind enough to allow me to photograph their paper treasures: Glenn Bray, Murphy Darden, Jack Devere, Mitch Diamond, Frank Driggs, Ted Fox, John Gray, Bruce Hershenson, Anthony Kisch, Jay Levine, Frank Newlin,

Steven Rebello, Larry Richards, Jim Ridenour, Steve Schapiro, Bill Spicer, Warren "Shorty" Stanley, Gabe Taverney, Dave Thomson, Dawn Wheeler, Roy Windham, and David Zinsser. And second, the poster dealers and proverbial carrot danglers who knew when I couldn't say no: A. Rodney Albright, Don Angst, Gene Arnold, James Ashton, Eddie and Claire Brandt, Brian Bukantis, Camden House, Chisholm Prats Gallery, Cinema Graphics, Cinemonde, Dennis Clark, Morris Everett, Roger Fenton, John Hawkinson, Francis Hofstein, Ray Hutto, Peter Laing, Walter Latimer, Butch E. Ford, Bill Luton, Moe's Movie Madness, Clarence Moore, David Morgan, Jim Murray, Bill Neal, Brad Panelle, Paper Chase, Roger Paulson, Robert Pelot, Poster Emporium, Walter Reuben, R. Neil Reynolds, Sam Sarowitz, Dan Strebin, George Theofiles, and Robert Wherling.

And my editor, Elisabeth Dyssegaard, and publicist Michael Barson; thanks for that first great lunch. Finally to my research and production team of Larry Richards, Todd Talliaferro, Les Hunter, and Hank Kaplan, whose dedication and admiration for this genre became my good fortune.

All posters are from the John Kisch Collection unless otherwise noted. All photographs are by John Kisch except those for *The Emperor Jones, Keep Punching, Lucky Ghost, Bubbling Over, O'Voutie O'Rooney,* and *She Devil,* which were shot by Nick Springett.

—J.K.